SACRED STRAINS OF PRAISE

MICHAEL PARKER &

MICHAEL SHOEMAKER

Paper back ISBN-13: 978-1-946469-79-3
Hardcover ISBN-13: 978-1-946469-80-9

ShelteringTree.Earth, LLC Publishing
PO Box 973, Eagle Lake, FL 33839

Did you enjoy this book?

We love to hear from our readers.

Please visit the authors and photographer at
ShelteringTreeMedia.com

About the Cover
Photographer: Michael Shoemaker
Title of Piece: Cello
Location of Piece: Magna, Utah

DEDICATION

To my dear mother, Shana Le Parker, whose faith in the Lord
has been a balm of Gilead throughout my life.

M. Parker

To my children, may you always walk in God's love.

M. Shoemaker

MICHAEL PARKER & MICHAEL SHOEMAKER

CONTENTS

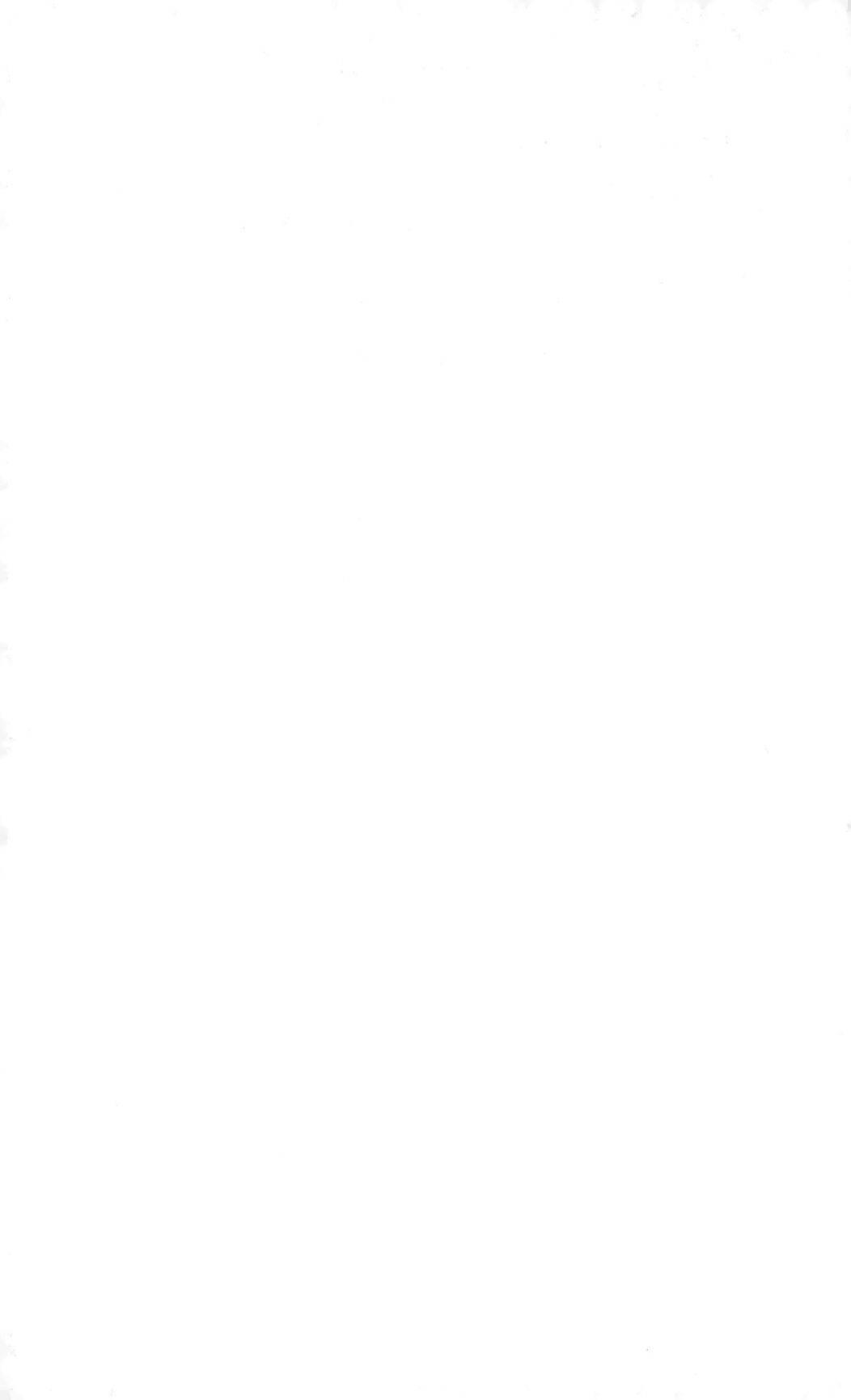

ACKNOWLEDGEMENTS

The authors would like to extend their gratitude to the editors of the following publications where these poems and photographs previously appeared, sometimes in different versions:

"Coming Out of Despair," by Michael Parker, *As Surely As The Sun,* Issue 2, September 2023

"Love" and "When Praying," by Michael Parker, *Literary Revelations Journal,* October 2023

"Allium Flower" and "Quaking Aspens," by Michael Shoemaker, *Littoral Magazine,* October 2024

"Leaves on the Sidewalk," by Michael Shoemaker, *The Amazine,* November 2024

"From Here to Eternity," by Michael Shoemaker, *Spirit Fire Review,* November 2024

"Sidewalk Art," "A Leaf On the Payment," and "From Here to Eternity," by Michael Shoemaker, *Pure In Heart Stories,* November 2024

"To a Christmas Angel, A Triptych" by Michael Parker, *PoetsArtists,* Winter 2011 Issue

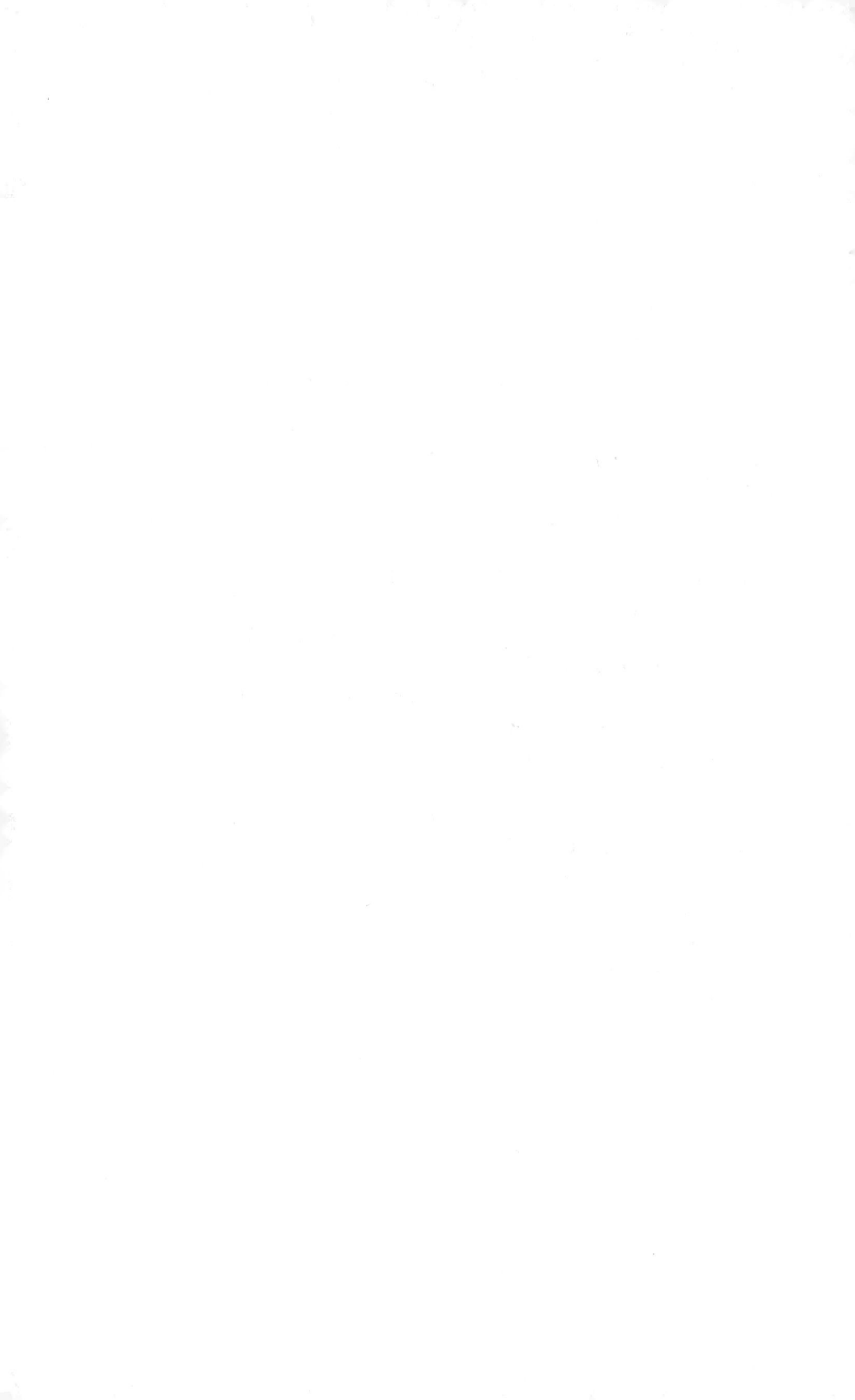

SEARCHING FOR GOD

MICHAEL PARKER & MICHAEL SHOEMAKER

HEAVENLY FATHER

Michael Parker

I've been anticipating Your arrival in my heart as I await
the arrival of my long-deceased Father in my dreams.

Ever since I felt that hope in me,
I always feel the need to go where I can find You.

Together, we build our relationship and love
like an empire withstands invasion like stone fights erosion.

Heavenly Father, how love envelopes me
as I carry Your name.

How I can hold a cusp of wind in my hands
like it was the tenuous and shallow breath of life.

How the land reaches its arms around the expanse like a hug
to calm the disturbance of the unsettled sea.

And, how You can clasp us all in your mind's eye
like the innumerable expanse of stars in the night sky.

This is the power of your name, Glorious and All-encompassing.

Will You settle down with me in my uncertainty?
Will You abide with me in my despair?

How I often yearn for the parcel of love
You have for me, intimate and sure.

I count the blessings that have come my way.
I count the small miracles that are heaven-sent.

Teach me. Lead me. Inspire me along the many paths
I travel in this boundless and unkind world.

Sometimes my words to You seem meaningless.
But You fill in the cracks of my humanness with gold and
meaning.

Heavenly Father, it's definitely love I carry for You.

CONSIDERING HOW WE CONNECT WITH GOD

Michael Parker

God's soft and halcyon voice
summons you to prayer.
It might be through a chime,
a song, a psalm, or a poem.

It might be at the church,
within the compass of your home,
in the confines of your office,
driving down the interstate,
working on the farm,
or while hiking in the temple
of the mountain.

Open the stage of your soul.
Speak from your heart.
It doesn't take a bounteousness
of thought.

The heavens will unfasten.
The soft petals of your mind
will spread.
And the capacity of your heart
(like the levels of a lake)
will expand and rise

permitting the compassionate God
to reveal Himself and speak.

TANKA OF PRAISE

Michael Shoemaker

sunflowers soak in warmth
from the white sky and noon sun
breezes stir from the south
raising fervent praise to the Creator
of earthworms and blue whales

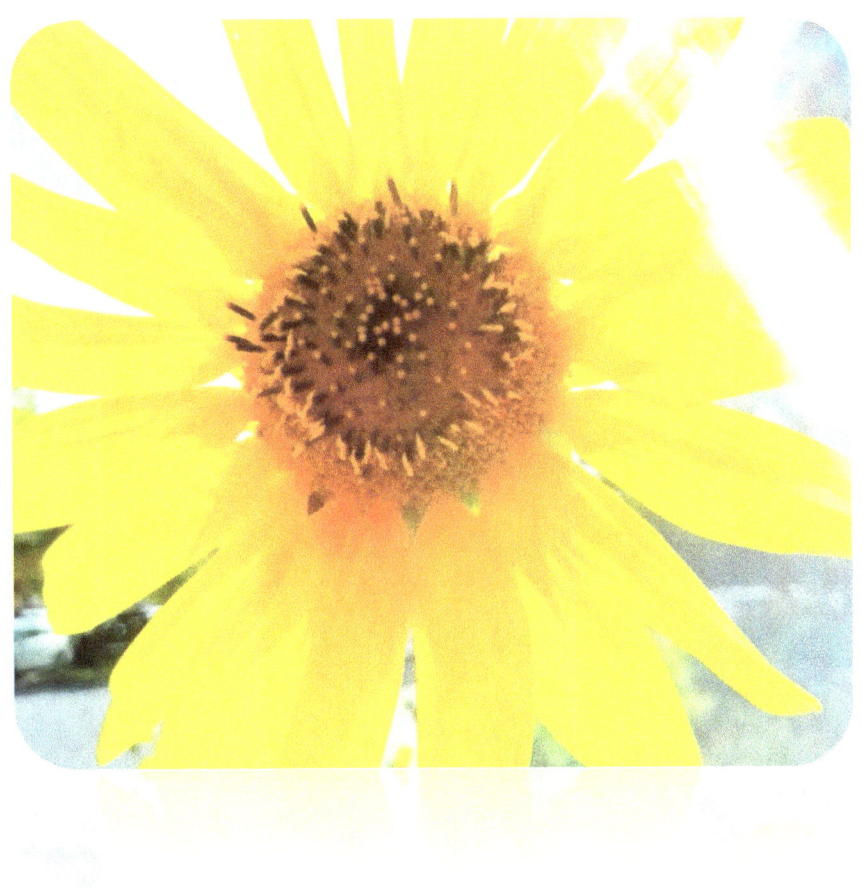

"Sunflower and Sunlight." Photography by Michael Shoemaker

WHEN PRAYING

Michael Parker
after Mary Oliver

I have a vision in my mind of Jesus
kneeling in front of His followers, His knees
grounded like a Shepherd's tree,
the roots extending hundreds of feet
underground.

His heart is formidable like a mountain,
its purpose etched into the walls of His heart:
"Thy Kingdom come, Thy Will be done."

The thoughts of my own mind soar in flight,
like a murmuration of starlings flying
in the wild season's breezes under
the ethereal foundations of heaven.

I speak words of gratitude
gracefully, penitently, as I consider
the voice of a young David exhorting
"enter His gates with thanksgiving
and His courts with praise," and
the Lord's apostle Paul admonishing
"give thanks in all circumstances,"
and declare "thanks be to God
for His indescribable gift!"

Then, finally, I listen for the quiet voice
in life's song or in the whirlwind's whisper
startling this life-worn soul
awake.

HAIKU

Michael Shoemaker

simple innocence
awe and wonder
— God's healing power

BE STILL, AND KNOW THAT I AM GOD

Michael Parker

Be still, and know that I am God: I will be exalted among the heathen, I will be exalted in the earth. (Psalm 46:10, AKJV)[1]

Though the earth may shudder and shake, convulsing in twain;
the tsunami flood the lowlands, inundating and unmooring
    everything in its path;
the tornado obliterate swaths of croplands and towns,
    leaving brokenness in its wake;
the hurricane embroil the sky into a maelstrom
    of violent and sonorous winds and rain
    annihilating everything it reaches;
or, the forest fire incinerate anything in its path
    as if touched by hell's flames, red and gold,
    as if sheaths of the sun's inferno ravaged there;
be still, and know that I am God.

Though bullies may deride you;
worry overtake you;
the path of life become too overwhelming;
your unending trials seem to block
    the passage home to God;
you feel you have committed too many wrongs
    to ever be accepted or loved by God;
the crucible of unyielding tribulations
    seem too much to bear;
fear of the future grip you;
or, the duplicity of the adversary seems
    to ensnare and imprison you;
be still, and know that I am God.

---

[1] All Scripture herein comes from the **Authorized (King James) Version (AKJV)**
KJV reproduced by permission of Cambridge University Press, the Crown's
patentee in the UK.

One might ask out of humility or despair
    what are the ways to be still?
How can one learn to know for themselves
    that He is God?
I can only share what has helped me:

Find a quiet place.
Pray to God for strength and navigation.
Look to the horizon of heaven.
Attend worship services.
Read the good Word of God.
Be thankful for your many blessings.
Remember God's plan.
Surrender to God.
Search out peace.
Remember, oh remember
    God is always with you.

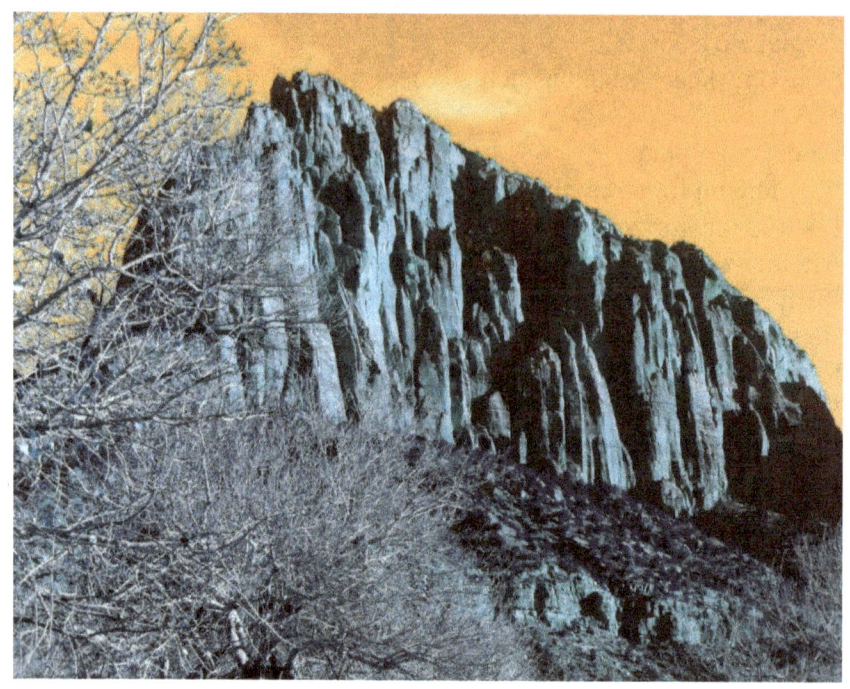

"Zion's Canyon Entrance." Photography by Michael Shoemaker

AVARICE OFF THE END OF THE PAGE

Michael Shoemaker

The love of money

is so pervasive

that it seems

to live

in every

cell wall

in every

galaxy spinning away

as the space

between God and us

expands.

Avarice

is so

slippery it

oozes out

of fingers

and sometimes

completely

meanders

off the end of the

PASSING ON GLEANED WISDOM AND A PRAYER

Michael Parker

WISDOM FOR THE DISCIPLE

Discern and discover the path you want to travel on
imbued by the light of Christ your soul desires to follow.

Cheer on, guide, and assist the weary along this marathon of life
for there will be multitudes who need you.

Extract enmity from your heart's core so the scrim
of resentment and animosity drops from your eyes
and you see everyone's glowing worth.

All who walk the journey of discipleship and self-efficacy learn
every hardship and suffering, every ounce of opposition,
a fathering God does recognize and know.

He bestows grace and leniency on those who show kindness and
love.

A PRAYER

Dear kind and all-knowing God, please be our forward guide
along the roughshod ways.

Allow the angels to attend us on our right hand and on our left;
and in our suffering, weaknesses, trials, and pain.

"Restore, restore," the fuel in our lamps that keeps us ready
for the bridegroom.

Remain forefront in our mind's eye so You are the focus
of our praises and our songs.

Our eyes are set on the golden halls of heaven, the journey's prize.
We know, like Job, kingdoms on high and kingdoms gleaming
    can be our rest and become our home through endurance
    on Your name.

Please bless us with the fortitude of sinew and bone,
    mountain, and the castle's keep
    to resist the devious stratagems
    of the adversary.

Reposit us now in Your good graces as we atone, recover
    from our flaws and vulnerabilities and follow Your will.

Help us see the miracles, the work of Your hands in all things.

What love we have treasured in our hearts of You, help us treasure
it anew.

Amen, and amen.

OUR KIND AND LOVING UNIVERSAL GOD: AN INVOCATION

Michael Parker

Our kind and loving universal God,
our hearts are laid bare to the wings
of Your influence. We approach You
at Your throne of stars, awestruck
by the abundance of beauty, grandeur,
and goodness You crown us with,
through the vast connectedness of this
the large and frangible human family.

As we walk the scenes of this wide expanse—
from the sheer rock face of the Oregon coast
to the burning white sands of Florida,
from the Rocky Mountains to rolling cornfields—
we pray our mouths and hands may be
the harbingers of peace.
We pray for a renaissance of love
a second Enlightenment that will
help confirm our aim as all-embracing poets.
We pray to be more affectionate and forgiving,
that we may heal, and our souls be healed.
We pray for a flourishing of tenderness and light.
We pray for all the inhabitants of the world
that when the cyclones have passed by us
there may be harmony growing
in our hearts like vines.

May we be united in consciousness and adoration.

We are grateful for the gift of sensibility.
We are grateful for our health
that buoys our ability to serve one another,
to adore one another. Forever and infinite
in the arms of your grace, Amen.

HOW CAN I REACH YOU?

Michael Shoemaker

How can I reach you, Dear Father of mine

so kind, generous and sublime?

I mindlessly peddle envy, contempt and hate

and every day on You for mercy I wait.

How can I understand Your love so divine

never ending in my heart intertwined?

How can I see what You see in me

when I treat others so treacherously?

And yet…And yet…when I look out at night

and through the stars You slowly turn each page of Your delight,

creation's consolation makes me whole and fills me with light.

I know, I know, something felt that I cannot deny.

I love You and on You I will always rely

for You sent Your best Son to expiate

and with the jailer's key, He sets me free.

LIFE'S ENDURING JOURNEY

BESIDE THE STILL WATERS

Michael Shoemaker

When I was laid off from my job,
I learned that fears can have teeth.
Eventually, God sent me
another job sufficient for my needs.

When I was rejected by others at school,
I learned the deep dark bowl of loneliness,
only to find that God's Beloved Son
sang comfort to my soul and sent a new friend.

When I was persecuted for His name's sake,
to the point I was threatened with non-existence,
I found His Holy Spirit gave me courage and utterance,
and His holy angels standing by me as a defense.

When I couldn't read and was ashamed,
I discovered door after door banged in my face.
He brought me a gift of hope
and called this present a loving-kindness a "teacher".

As the weather clouds roll in and my bones ache badly,
when I find that the pain will not go away,
there are times when I pray
and He cradles and rocks me
in His most able arms.
I know then I am loved,
never forgotten,
cherished and
finally, still,
completely stilled,
beyond understanding.
He is never beyond reach.

COMING OUT OF DESPAIR

Michael Parker

The Lord reveals I've been surrounded by His gleaming sanctuary.
I see I've been enveloped in the Lord's luminous light.

His grace empowers me like the sun that governs the day.
Hope is a constant baptism from God's Holy Spirit.

I look up and see heaven's perfect sky.
Invoking each of the Lord's names awakens me.

I no longer run out of prayers.
I am no longer forsaken like a leper.

The Lord prepares me in His glory.
The Lord reveals to me life's lambent humanity.

The living waters of the Lord fill me like a sea.
The good Samaritans walk with me along the path back to Him.

The birds of the sky fill my soul with His hymns.
I suddenly see the miracles, the miracles, the miracles.

THE VISIT WITH MY PSYCHIATRIST

Michael Parker

Every six months I visit my psychiatrist
to talk about how I am feeling based on
the events that have transpired in and around
my life since we last met. My psychiatrist
often offers solace and gives advice
on ways I can live a more meaningful life.
Lastly, we discuss the medications
I am taking and whether or not he needs
to increase dosages or change medications
that better help me cope with the throes
of anxiety and the claws of despair.

Today, he asked me if I was doing anything
in my life that helps me to better overthrow
the pangs of anguish that bring darkness
melancholia, or sometimes even
the despondency from living with
chronic pain. "As I have mentioned
in prior visits," I replied, "I write
poetry to help me cope with
hopelessness."

He asked whether I was able to write
over the last six months and whether
this has helped bring me peace
from the depression that falls on me
like an enemy. "Yes," I exclaimed.
"I am working on a project of new poems
with a good friend that we want
to publish. The process has been
a balm of hope for me."

He then advised that it was important
I find, have, and be able to feel grace
through my gift of expressing
what is vital in my life. He then
spoke about the etymology
of the word *grace*, that in Hebrew
it means *khen*. *Khen*, pronounced
"hen" while clearing your throat
a little at the word's beginning,
is the word that means grace,
delight, elegance, or inducing
a favorable response.

"In ancient Hebrew past,"
my psychiatrist said, "tribes
of families would set up tents
in a circle so that they would
create a wall of protection."

"Within the confines of this circle,"
he continued, "the rule of law was this—
that one another would treat each other
with respect and compassion, and
to be gracious to others by showing
favor, delight, charm, and beauty."

"Similarly," my psychiatrist confided,
"your mission in life is to use your gift
of poetry to show grace. As it says
in Proverbs: 'a gift is as a precious stone
in the eyes of him that hath it....' You receive
grace by writing about your pain
and you show grace by inducing
a favorable response or by giving
beauty, elegance, or charm
to others through your words."

All the way home, and throughout the night,
I thought about the meaning and
concept of grace. Not only had I agreed
to be and to show grace in my writing,
but I had consented to live a more
gracious life—to influence the family
tribe that encircles me, protects me,
shows compassion, and
who loves me and to make sure
each word I write will bring about grace
in the community of readers who,
like beloved loves, will open their mouths
and read the fallen petals of my poems
with rooted adoration and profundity.

MAXINE AND IRENE

Michael Shoemaker

They were co-conspirators
enveloped in anonymity.
They retired around the same time.
One taught swimming at the local pool.
The other cooked at the elementary school cafeteria.
A decade later, their husbands passed away.
Their common weekly activities were
playing Rummikub every Thursday night
at 7 p.m., with four other women,
going to the supermarket every Tuesday
and sitting next to each other at church each Sunday.
These were their apparent and unobscured activities.

Maxine loved to sew blankets.
Irene loved to shop for fabric and fringes.
Let's admit it, she liked fringes the best.
I was the leader of their congregation.
They enlisted me in their cloaked plans.
Thinking back, it was quite simple.
They were determined that no baby
in our neighborhood get cold.
As a team, they would provide blankets
for babies and I would give one to every
family with a baby that I visited.
It worked.
I always had four blankets in the trunk
of my car.
One year, I gifted fifty-six blankets,
one for every week of the year.
I knew Maxine and Irene had other
(perhaps more reliable)
distributors of blankets
which meant that before their deaths,
the two, sent out thousands

like pine tree seedlings carried in the wind
any direction they would take,
a blessing for generations to come.

I still wipe a tear away
thinking of Maxine's funeral viewing
when Irene covered her feet
with a baby blanket
— lots of fringes.

A FEAT OF CHARITY AT CHRISTMAS

Michael Parker

Let love be without dissimulation. Abhor that which is evil;
cleave to that which is good. Be kindly affectioned one to
another with brotherly love; in honour preferring one
another.... (Romans 12:9-10)

It was the Christmas season of 1989.
The sky had opened over us and dropped
the most snow our city had seen in more than a decade.
My Father had been out of a job for months
so he and his close friend started
their own accounting company.
We moved out of the house we were renting
and moved into their three-bedroom basement
that they turned into an apartment,
so both families could save money.

Thanksgiving came and went and it was obvious
to my parents that they did not have enough money
to buy gifts for all of their eight children for Christmas.
My parents called a family meeting to let us know.
"Instead of purchasing gifts for all of us," my Father said.
"How about we give Christmas to a family
who needs it?"

My dad knew the perfect candidate
for our charity—a young family of four
(Father, Mother, and two kids under five)
new to the neighborhood, who had just started
attending our congregation and were equally
struggling to meet their needs. Though it would be hard,
we agreed to my parent's plan. It would be a Christmas
of giving rather than receiving.

I don't remember the types of gifts or toys we bought
this family but I do remember wrapping them up in festive
Christmas wrapping. And late on Christmas Eve,
my parents and us kids piled into our trusted
Ford Econoline van, each of us holding the wrapped gifts,
and drove to the humble house of this poor family.
We parked down the street so we could drop off our gifts,
ring the doorbell, and run back to the van without
being seen. This act of charity had to remain anonymous
to be successful.

And it was.

A SOUL FULL OF STARS

Michael Parker

Today, I am a soul full of stars.
When night awakes and across the canopy
its candles are lit all by themselves,
stars align to show us pictures
not unlike the dreams that show us visions
and at this late hour, even our bones burn bright
with the knowledge of beautiful things to come.

What I love is a heaven revealed to me
like feeling the coming of light on my skin,
the warmth of it all, making known
I am a fellow citizen who fantasizes about
kindness and adoration in a country I hope
is fed on the bread of compassion, dressed
in shining brilliance.

I am no longer lonely.
I no longer despair.
I long for a world that detests fight or fire.
I yearn for a world that sings peace
ringing as high as the clouds
where I am surrounded by like-minded souls
all of us arrayed in Love's clothes.

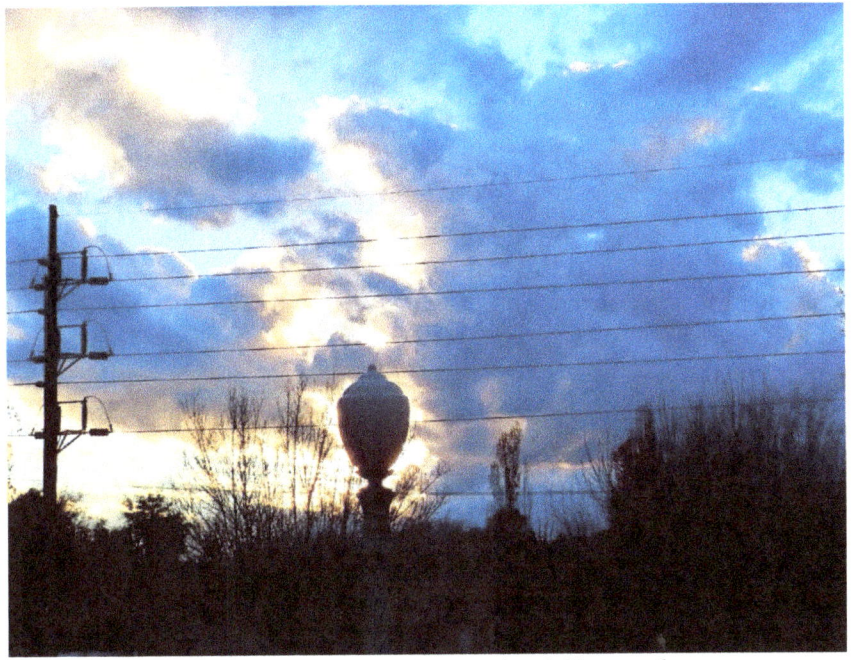

"In the Twilight." Photography by Michael Shoemaker

ON KNOWING

Michael Shoemaker

Words are inadequate to describe the path, but something can be said about the journey to knowledge. Disparate items or ideas present themselves to your mind. They are out in the open to view as if they were lying on a swap meet table ready for purchase. However, they are so different they do not belong on the same table, at the same swap meet, or even at the same market. Carefully, metaphorically, you pick them up, turning them over in your mind's hands and come to know them. You observe them in motion and at rest. There is no cataloging, classifying, or pretending that they are more basic or simple than they are. There is no taking in of the oxygen of one item or idea before experiencing its liveliness manifested and absorbed by your senses. You welcome it to your mind like an invited and honored guest asking yourself, "What is the essence of this one among many? How does it exist and continue to exist?" No timeline or master microwave clock dings to tell you what you are cooking is done and when to move on. It is a feeling, a sense of soulful satiation that releases you to go on to other items and ideas. Even after a thorough, vivid, and tireless inspection, it is not unusual for confusion and frustration to set in like dense fog as you go through a nearly unsolvable maze. At these times, you can pray to God for deliverance and there are times when you are delivered and the fog rises enough for you to see one foot in front of the other making it possible for you to walk on. Previously undetected patterns between and among items and ideas can come to your mind in a single lightning strike of thought or a more rhythmic fashion as the tidal waves ebb and flow along the seashore. At other times, it may come as a visual presentation into your mind that shows the relatedness and togetherness of what you have been pondering in proper form like the helix of a strand of DNA. At the end of this activity, you are more invigorated, nearer to God and are carried to a higher mountain where you can see and perceive new paths never previously conceived, perceived, or believed.

As you end one journey of knowledge, receiving more understanding than when you first started, you stand at a peak and on firmer ground. Ready to apply your new knowledge, you walk forward, equipped for the next quest.

HOW MY PARENTS INSTILLED GRATITUDE IN THE FAMILY

Michael Parker

In order to keep peace in the house
and instill a semblance of gratitude
among our large family, my parents
occasionally gathered us (eight children strong)
into the living room and invited
each of us to take turns going around
the room saying something nice about
each member of the family.
Father and Mother started and set the tone
by elaborating on a characteristic
they most adored about each child
and the other spouse. What started
as a "do we have to do this?" affair
turned into a tender, thoughtful
examination of the colorful threads
that wove the fabric of our family
together. Hearts were softened.
Voices cracked from emotion.
Eyes grew moist and teary.
And many of us, even the boys,
took after our mother,
and quietly wept.

Forty years older, and five years
since the passing of my Father,
I cherish those times as if they were
the glue that kept us united and in tune.
And though we have had to work
on our own familial relationships
like any modern family,
I can't help but celebrate the
acumen of inspired parents.
They nurtured the seed that has grown
into a strong oak.

WATERS BEFOULED

Michael Shoemaker

...and let them have dominion over the fish of the sea, and over the fowl of the air. (Genesis 1:26)

I spoke with a member of the Navajo nation
and asked what they fish for in their
creeks, streams and rivers on the reservation.

He shook his head with a frown, "Catfish is all that is left.
We used to catch and eat, now we catch and release.
After the Gold King Mine spill we don't
take or eat anything from our waters."

I sing to you, *Animas River* (Spanish for 'River of Lost Souls')

Where have all the bald eagles gone
now that there are no fish to eat?
Where is the giving and the taking
when the taking has killed what you
live to give so freely?

Where have the clear eyes gone
that now only stare in horror
grief and disbelief into orange
waters passing us all by,
but only seen
by these
people?

LEARNING LOVINGKINDNESS

Michael Parker

Follow the path of love as shown by the living Jesus.
Consider kindness as a power and intensity, not as a weakness.

Consider how others have assisted or inspired you.
Cultivating gratitude is like the sun breaking through a storm.

Seeing the expression on another person's face in the moment of
giving service is vital.
Be available and approachable with a mindset to make a difference.

Smile. Shake a hand. Visit the ill. Make a meal. Let another go
before you.
Help someone. Watch someone else's children. Drive someone to
the store.
Raise the weary hands that hang down and the feeble knees.

Realize most everyone is on a search for meaning and happiness.
See the good of your life cross over the wide sea of the sky.

Love those you meet, befriend, or serve.
Raise others' spirits from the depths of life's harsh realities.

See others in their most perfect state—as children of God.
See others for what they are worth—as pure love.

Help others see the beauty of their soul.
Remember what you share inspires someone's kindness.

Share a part of your day with another person.
Be kind to and lift those who are on a different path than yours.
Never pass judgment on someone. Walk a mile in their shoes.

Meditate and pray, keeping the face of others on the revolving stage
of your mind.

Reflecting on others in this manner can be a powerful moment of transformation.

Listen to the downtrodden. Include others who seem to be left out. Praise others. Refrain from speaking ill of another soul.

Practice giving one act of selfless kindness a day.
Keep trying. Every generous motion engenders kindness.

HALF RENGA

Michael Shoemaker & Michael Parker

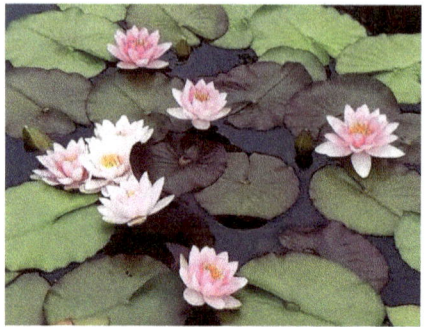

"pink water lilies." Photography by Michael Shoemaker

prayers are pink water
lily petals reaching high
skyward blue

> *serene words, peaceful refuge*
> *spring's heart-to-heart communion*

some say prayer is
the Christian's native air
and gasp the words now

> *"Thy Kingdom come and will be*
> *done," arises from our hearts*

"Thy faithfulness is
great," our hymns of praise
stretching out unto Thee

> *sensing the bright shade of peace*
> *feeling the contours of hope*

prayers are oxbow streams
filtering souls—giving
habitat for life

small piece of heaven on earth
and love from the Lord's outreach

Oh Father, Thou hast
heard us on pinnacles and
deep in ferny bogs

on turquoise oceans and seas
in the suburbs and cities

on sweaty bus seats
in distressing interviews
in idle airports

in hectic days, sleepless nights
in humble meditations

in hospitals'
echoing corridors
suing for peace

even in protestations
and our kind affirmations

prayer is a humble
caged sinner's plea
freed to saints' rejoice

the appeal of the beggar,
the depressed, or in despair

pray always
continuance in prayer
pray always

ask, seek, knock: you will receive
find, and it will be opened

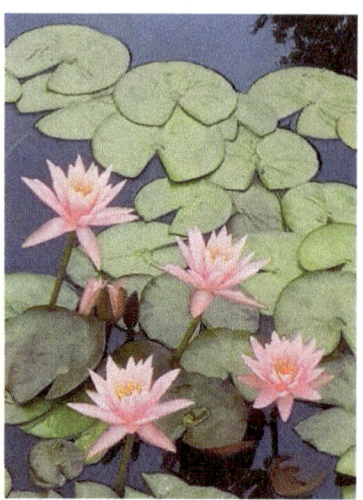

"four water lilies." Photography by Michael Shoemaker

ONE-MAN FIRING SQUAD

Michael Shoemaker

I won't, I won't, and you can't make me.
You command me to raise my rifle
and assassinate my character
by lying, stealing, cheating, adultery and murder
claiming apologetically that these are the only crops
that will grow now in this wicked, old, rocky and worn soil.
I will starve and perish long before
you will hear the click of my gun
as the trigger is pulled back in deep self-betrayal.
No, I won't, and you can't make me.

KEEP A BRIGHTNESS OF HOPE

Michael Parker

In the world ye shall have tribulation: but be of good cheer; I have overcome the world. (John 16:33)

1

After the torrential rains, after the storm surge
six feet deep from the once-in-a-lifetime storm,
rare and one-of-a-kind prayers flood the heavens.
God will grant an answer, furnish the skies
with a holy dove carrying a branch full
of olive leaves. Peace permeates loving hearts.
Hope is as bright as the new sun.

2

Sometimes we might forget or fail to appreciate
that Jesus, who wears the stripes and scars
from the tree of Golgotha, knows the suffering
and discomfort of a singular man who is losing
the capacity to draw into his lungs full breaths
like full moons. Not enough oxygen to sustain
the body's main organs. Yet, the man has never
forgotten Christ knows his pain, tenfold.
The man's faith shines like a morning.

3

Unshakeable belief. Blessed assurance.
Conviction. Aspiration. Longing for
a radiant future and a consecrated life.
Dear friends, Jesus is the sacrificial lamb.
He has overcome all. In Him, we are
redeemed, glory be to God.
No more sorrowful depressions.
Strength to withhold temptations.
Greater love to obey Jesus.
Resilience that becomes our city
on the hill. Yes, friends in Christ,
keep a brightness of hope.

TO A CHRISTMAS ANGEL, A TRIPTYCH

Michael Parker

1
I forget you
exist, laid out
(caringly)

inside your long
box, the measurements
suited just right for

sustained storage.
Odd that it is only now
we remember

you are with us, always
in our home, you and
the other treasures.

But especially you,
winged creature. For a
holy paramour

of paradise,
so used
to arriving through

punctured skies,
the sparkle of
heaven's foundation

accentuating
it all,
to not fly in

at all,
but to be unearthed

from layers

of dusty
containers, from
the dark place

under the stairs.

2
The gathered fabric of the winter storm cannot hide or impede you.
You will always arrive with the message in your fixed eyes, on
your lips, and in your outstretched hands.

You are not the type to wrestle with sinners or strike down eighty-
five thousand in the camp of the enemy. Those are the ilk of John's
apocalyptic angels, hearts always set on vengeance and war.

You are the Good Tidings attendant: peacemaker, steward, full of
cherubic innocence. I catch just one gaze on your effulgent
expression, that slight lean of the head, and I see Botticelli's
Aphrodite, that same mask of immaculateness beaming like a
morning. Oh, to always be arriving in such a state and glory.

Would you believe, after so many seasons, you draw me in like no
other? Turn me inside and make me search for things that are
neither tangible nor real?

You carry such a sway. You minister such a hope.

3
You are present with me, fighting against the weight of the raven-
colored robes of night. I am by the window. The cold air,
indomitable in its mission, has breached the glass and I struggle for
warmth. I doubt you are equally affected.

Should I tell you the problems of the world, that the lowly
shepherds on the hillside (the ones who are always most open to

the message of glowing people with wings) are living in my neighborhood? Not literally, of course, but you understand. It is cloaked in the word "lowly".

There is a young couple who can't bear children, even though their dreams are populated with them. There is a father out of work who questions his worth. There is an infant with a hole in her heart. There is a young man torn asunder from the bullying at school. There is a grandfather who is having ongoing treatment for cancer. And then there is the most of us, looking into the face of our finances, but only seeing the threads of disintegrating leaves, substance(less) snowflakes.

If you would talk, you might say blessings come after the trials, that joy is keener having known the sorrow. That's all fine, I say. But what of hope while in the thick of it? How do I own it? And how do I fire it up in the down-turning?

You, dear seraph of the Classic Angel Collection, have twenty more days to teach me this before you're off to your heaven under the stairs.

CHRISTMAS ON THE MOVE

Michael Shoemaker

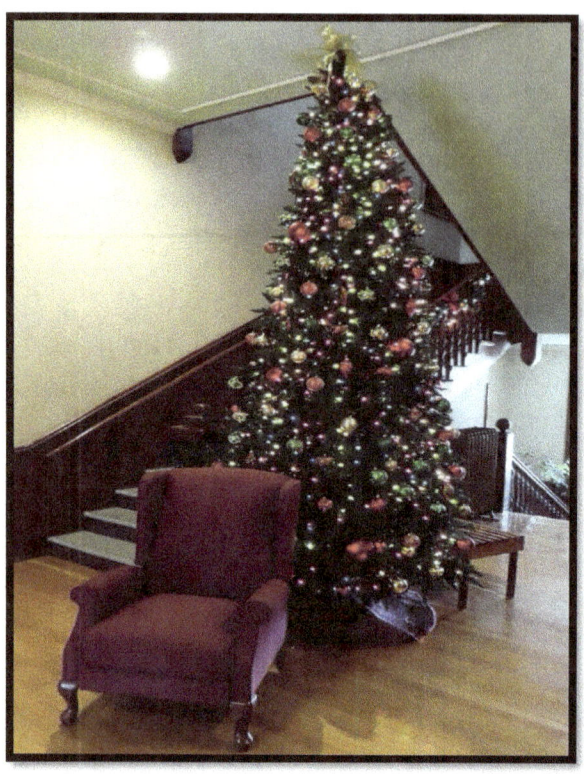

"Christmas Tree." Photography by Michael Shoemaker

Jesus's ministry moves.
Even as a baby
he was Egypt
and then Calvary bound,
now, to the Second Coming.

How can we expect
Christmas not to be
on the move
and in the air?

I was hundreds of miles from home
down, lonely, tapped out, nothing left.
My prayer was all
I could breathe
through trembling tears,
"Father, help me."

There was a knock on my door.
I opened it to Steve's warm smile.
My friend from home gave a huge hug.
I spoke. He listened and listened.
He prayed a blessing. I listened.
Holy peace enveloped us
in God's blanket
He offers freely
to All.

This year Christmas
is on the move
in each of us.

THE SHEPHERD ON THAT MOMENTOUS MORNING

Michael Parker

The air holds its frail breath—
dew laces the fields on the hills
in the quiet of early morning
and the stars, like quiet pilgrims,
gather around the brightness
of the New Star.

I am only a shepherd,
but even my dog lifts her head,
ears set to attention,
tilted to something unseen,
maybe a hymn stitched into the wind.

The glowing angels who hung
in the sky bearing peace and joy
and tidings of great wonders
of a Christ-child laying
in a manger in Bethlehem
have gone now.

Oh, to be chosen—
not for wisdom, nor wealth,
but for the smallness of being,
the simplicity of watching
over God's small creatures,
and listening.

I walk to the town in earnest,
the wild grass making my feet wet,
and there (as the angels foretold)
in a lowly stable—a child,
radiant as morning,
cradled in the arms of a mother

who looks at him
as though she has known him forever.

Do you feel it too?
This joy that bends stiffened knees,
this light that sings in the bones?

Let the concourses of angels come
their voices breaking through
the fabric of the sky
and flooding the heavens.
Let the beasts lay round about
their breaths like ardent prayers.
For even the earth, like me—
broken, unholy, wounded—
seems to have waited ages
for this sacred moment
to break forth in joy
to finally be redeemed.

LIFE'S FINAL JOURNEY

Michael Parker
for my Father

Around the beautiful Eden of your beingness,
the furrowed face of the cornfield.
The bright swords of sunbeams.
The firestones that hold in the flames.
The many extended miles of aspirations
and the many long days filled
with pain and endeavor.

At the end of this journey,
the vast wide river of life expels you
onto the luminous shore of everlastingness
where the white-robed oracle guarding
the iridescent gates will whisper its riddle.

Being like a god, you know the answer.

The gift, because of your knowledge,
is the entrance to a great and strange place
glowing like the light of the brightness of stars
with a key to a heaven-like mansion
where there are rooms lined with books
full of wisdom and light,
and the overwhelming awareness of love,
emanating, as if arriving on the wings
of a flight of birds.

Here you will reside.
Here you will build rooms for your progeny,
who will arrive arms wide open
time after time and again
like new mornings.

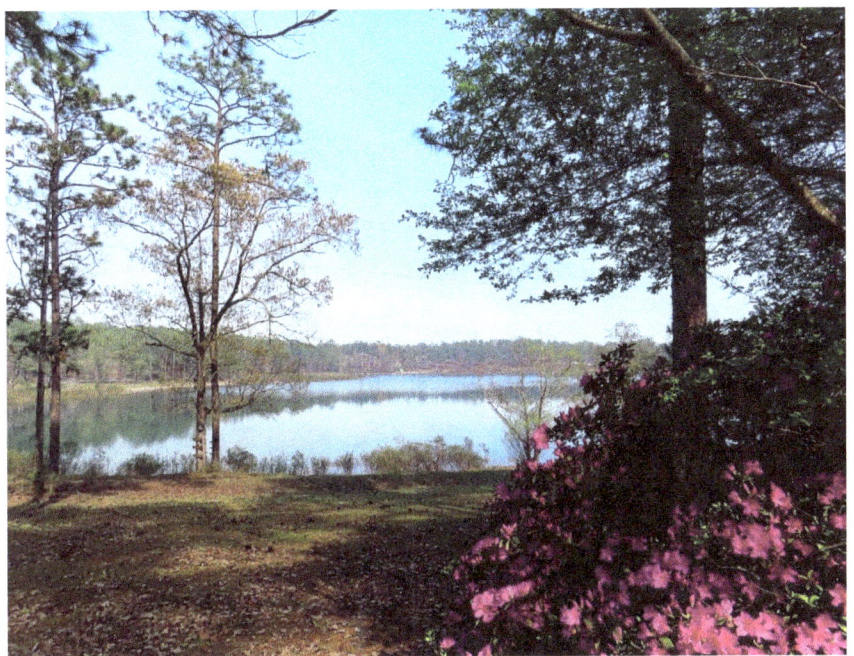

"Blue Lake Is Calling." Photography by Michael Shoemaker

LOVE
Michael Parker

watching side-by-side the infinitude of light
burst from the iridescent sunset

the marriage of complimenting luminaries
kissing under a resplendent blanket of stars

cultivating the garden of another's soul
yielding its fruit together at harvest time

feeling the sparks flying inside our souls
like the electricity flowing between two hearts

hearing the words adoration, devotedness,
ardency, and confidant

how an investment is a great metaphor
for our burgeoning relationship

the encouragement we award one another
the charity we impart to a fellow traveler of life

the buoyant meditations and singing bowls
which ring out the pure tones of our tenderness

the language of compassion and harvests—
beneficent words borne with holiness

and you and I rediscovering one another
as we transverse through our own Garden of Eden

SITTING IN THE CHAPEL

Michael Shoemaker

Steepled silence,
framed arches,
dedicated grounds,

bailed hay,
placed respectfully
during construction
in a Sunday School classroom
to prevent freezing
of the cement floor
while curing.

Not just a place
to play basketball
or learn about family finances
or to spy Aspen leaves
spinning in the wind
through stained-glass.

My church is a portal
of peace, a place
to resolve, a window
of faith, knowledge,
and reflection,
una pileta de amor
(a pool of love.)

THE PRIEST'S HOLY HOMILY
Michael Parker

The Priest's holy homily guided me to the moon.
His rousing voice aiming me toward this vision;
the moon's bone-bleached white blinding me,
as I grew close and then assisting me in
a symbolic landing.

I was astonished to be able to take breaths
like full moons hearing language so beautiful,
and the hint of lavender, talc, and incense
in the chapel stunned my sense of smell.

I am weightless as a bird, my wings spread wide
to hold me up, give me momentum. Yet, I am
a study of faith in slow motion.

Beckoned to a wasteland, could I withstand
the devil's duplicity throughout my time
in the wilderness as Christ accomplished?
My lack of devotion disheartens me.

Can the bestowing of the bread of the Lamb
and wine for consecration make me whole?
If so, I would be able to push through
the despair of life's suffering; the sound of
my communal relief a sacred mantra for
this barren place.

The words responding to the voice of God is
like an eclipse and I am jettisoned back
to this clouded Earth to sit in awe, basking
in the glory of the heavenly text

and the light and grace that has sanctified
this spent man.

HAIKU

Michael Shoemaker

veterans' memorial park
starlings dispel
trumpet plays "Taps"

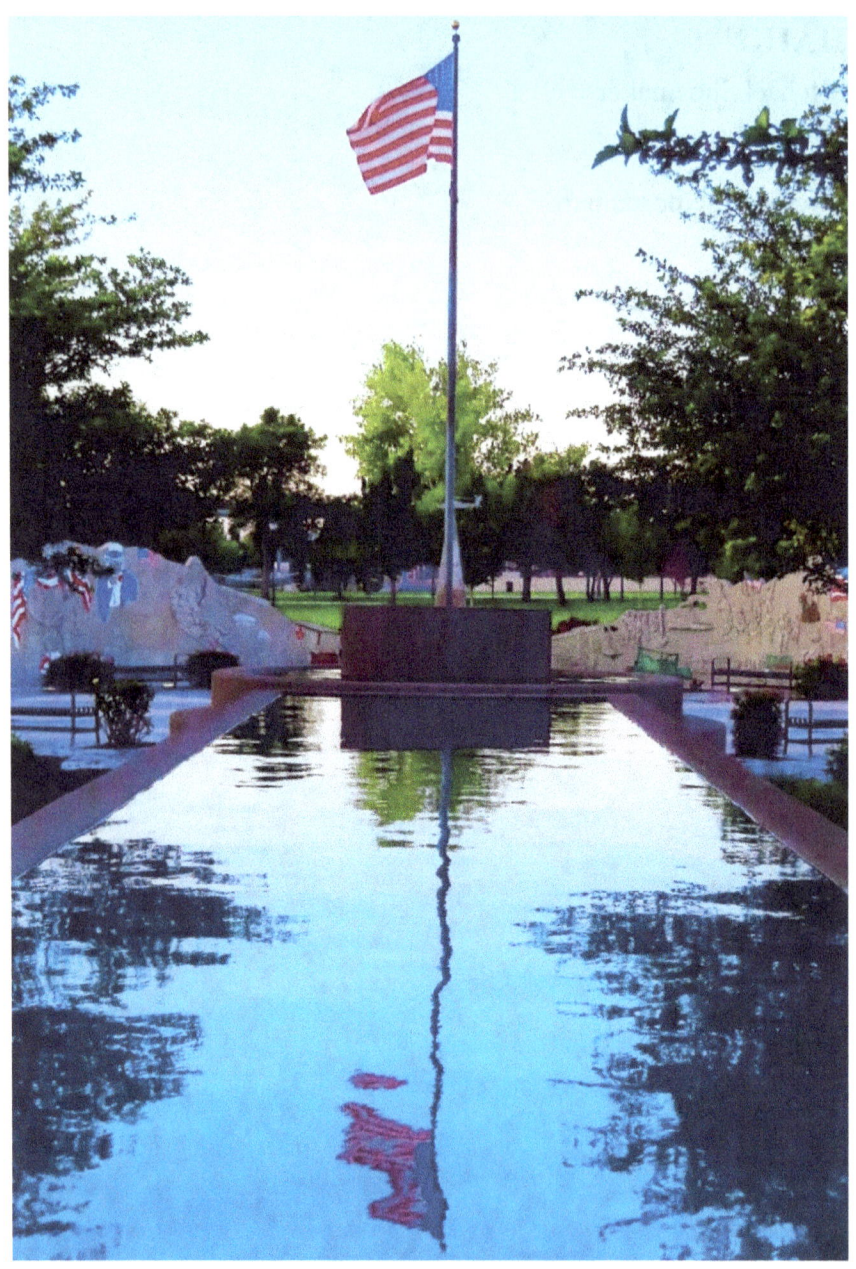

"Veterans Memorial Park." Photography by Michael Shoemaker

MY FAITH

Michael Parker

I abide in the household of faith. //Faith as the well I was drawn from. Faith as the fresh headwaters I drink from. I no longer thirst. //Boundless supplies of faith have followed my tender-hearted prayers. I shine by faith. Faith, the constellations I was born under; faith, the blanket I sleep under; and faith, the anchored foundation of my history, glowing gold. //Thoughtful. Buoyant. Enlivened. Galvanizing. The comforting wings of inspiriting faith hold me. //Faith, the Holy Spirit's instruction, and song. Faith that named me. Faith that fed me. Faith that raised me. Faith, my boyhood under a desert sun. Faith, the curtains of the rainstorm and the deluge of hope that follows it. I was a child of faith, a parable of faith, faith pressed into the palm of my hands like a river's stone. Before I could speak there was faith, before I could walk, the same. // "…faith is the substance of things hoped for, the evidence of things not seen." This is the tenet of my faith I long to live by. Faith roamed the desert paths like the children of Israel, in search of a homeland. //Faith found it in this awe-inspired and soul-weary man. //Faith is the unshakeable mountain. Faith is a face through the veil. Faith, the balm of Gilead I dress my wounds by. //The revelatory sunrays heralding faith I wrap around me like clothes. //My constant banner of faith I wave above my head for the home of my faith. Faith, like a standard of Zion. //Faith as sustaining as meat. Faith, my daily bread. // I have been nursed by faith. //Faith was my companion in the desert land of my youth. Faith was my companion on distant shores, teaching the children of God. A missionary fortified by the friendship of faith. And faith is my companion in the green valley of adulthood. //The boy once had a dream of faith and how faith is never lost if it is written upon the fleshy tablets of the heart. //I believe in that faith today. //All my days have been a lifeblood of faith. Faith the crown of heaven I wear upon my head. Faith, I place upon my shoulders like a King's robe. And faith, the revealed path I walk to find my way back home to God.

WHAT IS ETERNAL BLISS?

Michael Shoemaker

Most of the time, I do not recall or project eternity well. The earliest memory I can recall is drawing submarines in kindergarten at 5 years old. I was good at drawing submarines. It was a skill I have since lost. Projecting eternity is even more difficult. Next month's water bill, next week's work performance, and tomorrow's leftovers for lunch are often the best that I can project. The eternal present seems more approachable. Moments of love or pain can seem frozen in a block of eternal happiness or misery. My aperture or depth of field of eternity is so shrunken, that I can sometimes see only my shoelaces well enough to tie them. However, when I pray and study the Scriptures, my understanding of eternity expands just as heated air in a hot air balloon lifts it into the sky. There are cases where mothers can sense when a beloved child is in danger. Like these mothers, I believe in a God who knows me so intimately that He knows when I need His guidance. And I question less and less that God wants to show me more of eternity— past, present and future. Otherwise, how can I, as a mortal, know anything about my future grandchildren now?

Bliss, "perfect happiness or great joy," concerns me a bit. What new and different creature will I need to be to live contented with perfect eternal happiness? Will I have to surrender sarcasm or never again gulp of gossip? It seems a bitter pill to leave behind these familiar trappings. I have heard some say that they were so happy they could not speak. This has caused me to ask myself: what would eternal bliss or happiness be like? We may sometimes fantasize that heaven is a place where no one speaks, but as social beings, would we be honest enough to call this eternal bliss? As you can see, when I pass through the portals of mortal life, I may need one-on-one tutoring in the eternity learning lab to unlearn my earthiness and accept bliss for what it really is. But there is one thing I know—I will feel less lonely when I see your smiling face as you pass through that same door into eternity.

WHAT THE CHITTERING OF THE GRACKLES IN THE YARD REVEAL TO ME

Michael Parker

In this world where the negative and hateful shine,
you are the element that is positive.
You do not need to be heavy-hearted.
You do not need to walk the long valley of life
mouse-like, frightened of the predators in the sky,
or search out higher land because of the floods
coming from the monsoon.
You have the courage of a cougar, the bravery of a bear
hunting in the high valleys of the rugged mountains.
Fear not the test results showing lung disease.
All you need to do is breathe calmly through the pain,
the shortness of breath, and through the laborious day
and the cold, forsaken night.
Imagine yourself greater than you are, greater than
the limitations of your unceasing suffering,
like the interminable sea tides.
Yes, you carry within you the divine tenacity of God.
The spirit of love inhales and exhales within
the frame of your wide-open heart.
You know you are one with all the natural and
loving things, with family, friends, and carers.
Let go of negative emotions that no longer serve you.
Appreciate what is around you before the day wanes.
Reassess what is important to you. Sew love.
Plant hope. Look to the morning with new eyes.
Wherever you are along the sojourn, no matter
how lonely you feel in your suffering,
the winds call out to awaken your soul
to remind you over and over you are not alone.
You are a child of the Divine who knows
where you are and where you have been.
And if by chance the Fates happen to cut your string,
and you are taken away, there is another place

you will dwell just beyond the horizon
where death and misery are no more
and long-lost loved ones are there with open arms
wet faces, and joyous shouts
to welcome you home.

A MOMENTOUS OCCASION

Michael Shoemaker

The pump organ blurts out an indistinguishable glob of sound and fury, filling the air with dissonance and fate and causing churchgoers to sit bolt upright and the organist to murmur to herself, mortified "More practice, yes, needs more practice." The twins are already wrestling beneath the pews for the seating pole position. A teenager asks for two sticks of gum, one for after the first one falls flat and flavorless. The limp green-grey globe willow tree leans slightly left outside the stained-glass window in the churchyard; it waves greetings in the wind and catches one speck of clouds on its return, while baby chicks chase one another in ring-around-the-rosie fashion among overgrown blades of grass and drowsing tulips. The chorister braces her weight with both hands on the music stand with worry lines rising on her brow, but pioneer faith and courage bulge in her heart. The air conditioning rumbles and finally turns on. Two old men in wool three-piece suits pat one another on the back and then shake calloused hands, an outward expression of their covenant of neighborly kindness—the unsaid promise to stand by and help forever in bad times and good. Little is said, but much is meant. Someone sneezes widely, erasing a chalkboard of thoughts, reverence and reverie. She looks back from the front pew, smiling heaven's own guiding light.

I suppose one hears, sees, and knows all for one split moment when time stands still, contemplating a proposal of eternal marriage, sending chills up the spine.

THE GOATS AND THE BEES
Michael Parker

My Maori missionary companion and I were serving
the two branches of saints on the east and west sides
of the Coromandel Peninsula on the eastern frontier
of New Zealand, the Land of the Long White Cloud.

We were inspired to travel the hour and a half
from Tairua and over the asperous mountains
to Thames Valley, which sat at the foot of
the peninsula, to stay the night with
Sister Brown and her teenage son.

We began our stay by helping Sister Brown
with her grocery shopping. We then returned
to her humble two-bedroom home which sat
on a large plot of land where they grazed
two goats for milk and had a modest-sized garden.

While we were setting the table to eat dinner,
the goats began screaming, a loud, unholy noise.
Sister Brown told her son to quickly go out
to the paddock and check on the goats.
Within a minute, he returned crying out
"the goats are being stung!"

We ran out to the edge of the gated paddock,
where the two goats were chained to two posts
on top of a small hill. Immediately we could see
a large, impenetrable swarm of bees, dark against
the gray, winter sky, flying around the goats and
stinging them. The goats, in an act to free themselves
from their posts and from the bees, jumped
and kicked, their mouths stretched so wide from
screaming that they could have chewed up
the mammoth sky.

If we could only free the goats from their posts,
we thought, the goats could run away from the bees.
Sister Brown's son tried getting close, but the bees
started to swarm toward him so we called him back
from his attempts.

As a missionary, I thought I should do something—
call forth the heavens to intervene or cry out
to the bees to depart in the name of the Lord.
Surely such faith had been acted upon before
to bring about extraordinary miracles.
But I froze like a statue, unable to use
my priesthood to stop the bees or
send them off and away from their prey.
Each cry from the goats stung my soul
like an angry horde of bees.

We stood there for hours watching the goats,
which once bucked, jolted, and screamed,
until they settled and laid on the ground
crying and until their cries quieted
and they died. The relentless bees swarmed
around them well into the night
when we retired to the house
emotionally exhausted.

Nearly thirty-six years later my mind
is still pricked with guilt for not helping
the goats. It's as if I am a part of my very own
parable in which a man was invited to use
his spiritual gift to intervene in a tragic event,
but didn't. And because he didn't use his gift,
it was taken away by the Lord of the Gifts,
never again to be able to perform
the endowment of miracles
for the rest of his life.

TWO TANKAS

Michael Shoemaker

broadened horizons
petrels bullet into swells
wings awash in the sunset
carry home in faith's jet stream
— flourishing paths well-supplied

under the oak tree
our searching fingers reach out
leaves tumble freely
on one side apology
on the other forgiveness

IF THE WORD OF CHRIST DWELLS IN YOU RICHLY, SING

Michael Parker

Let the word of Christ dwell in you richly in all wisdom; teaching and admonishing one another in psalms and hymns and spiritual songs, singing with grace in your hearts to the Lord. (Colossians 3:16)

I remember when I was a teenager
visiting a friend for a week
during summer break
in Silver City, New Mexico,
when we drove to the hub of the city
Friday night and cruised Hudson Street.
Along the way, we had picked up
fellow friends and disciples of Jesus.
We filled to overflowing the cab and bed
of my friend's truck and as a choir
of modern-day angels sang our favorite
songs of praise to our Lord, trying
to sing over the din of hard rock
and country western songs blaring
out the open windows of hot rod cars
and trucks passing by. And the parade
of passing vehicles and passers-by
watching from the sides of the street
seemed to perk up and listen
as we sauntered by, our voices raised
in holiness to the Lord trying to
transform the large desert city
into a holy Sunday Service.
I daresay our hearts couldn't help
but explode within our breasts
as we sang with fervor and zeal
beloved hymns such as
"How Great Thou Art,"
"Amazing Grace,"
"How Firm A Foundation," and

"All Creatures of Our God and King."
We knew the Word was alive in us.
We knew the Holy Spirit knew
for we could feel it emanating
with us like a raging bonfire.
And even God, who seemed present
in the immense river of stars above us
knew we were witnesses of our Lord
in song and sacred hosannas.

HOW YOU LOVED LIGHTHOUSES

Michael Shoemaker

Mom, you left so suddenly
through the portals of death
it felt accidental, abrupt,
like you leaving mid-stream
except you always taught me
that God has a way,
He has a plan.

You loved lighthouses
more than they will ever deserve,
more than made sense.
From kitchen towels
to bathroom wallpaper
to my birthday cards you signed,
I still keep them on my desk.
They sweep the ocean's surface
in the dark— searching.

We had a plan to go on a trip
to visit nine lighthouses in ten days,
all deposits made, travel insurance paid,
but before we left
you had to go
and I had to remain.

This time, I took the trip anyway,
explaining my solo traveler status
to a couple on the bus
on their second honeymoon.

Not sure that we could meet
at Cape Hatteras Lighthouse Station
which looked out from land to surf to sea.
Sitting on a bench much too short

for my long legs, but perfect for yours,
I found you there sitting by my side,
as you promised.

The lilt, cry and noon-day glint
of a single seagull wing
and the light sea breeze caressed me
like your hand
that gently ran across the crown
of my domed bald head.

I know, I know, Mom,
you must go and I remain.
God has a plan,
He is the Way.
I trust Him, like you do.
It still hurts
every day.

THE PARABLE OF THE TEN VIRGINS

Michael Parker
for my Mother
Watch, therefore, for ye know neither the day nor the hour wherein
the Son of man cometh. (Matthew 25:13)

My mother and I were as close as a mother and son could be
during those formative teenage years. Many late nights and
early mornings, when the rest of the family were in a deep sleep,
you could find us stretched out across the couches talking about
life, the scriptures, or the Savior.

One night, after I had graduated from high school, the topic
of parables surfaced like fresh sea kelp on the shore. We briefly
talked about the men who multiplied their talents, placing new wine
in old bottles, the house that was built on rock and the other on sand,
about not hiding our candles under a bushel, the prodigal son,
the lost sheep, the good Samaritan, and the allegory
of the bread of life.

But it was the parable of the ten virgins my mom wanted to receive
my insights on. My mother, because of her good heart, naturally
thought
the five wise virgins were cruel for not sharing their oil with
the five unwise virgins. I don't remember my exact response, but
I knew the five wise virgins weren't being merciless or heartless by
refusing the pleas of the unwise virgins. I had perceived two things
about the wise virgins: they had lived their lives in such a way
they had stored more oil so they were prepared for the bridegroom's
arrival; and the second thing centered on the wise virgin's keen
awareness they would need to have extra oil in their lamps for
unexpected events, such as the long wait for the bridegroom and
the length of the marriage ceremony. They needed oil in their lamps
for both. Likewise, we need to live our lives where we are storing
up

the invaluable oil in our lamps by praying, studying the Scriptures, doing good to others, and obeying the commandments so the Lord

can say to us, "I know you. You may enter."

BEAUTY FOR ASHES

Michael Parker

> *To appoint unto them that mourn in Zion, to give unto them beauty for ashes, the oil of joy for mourning, the garment of praise for the spirit of heaviness; that they might be called trees of righteousness, the planting of the Lord, that he might be glorified.* (Isaiah 61:3)

You and I have never walked life's easy path.
Obstacles known to us as trials and tribulations
litter our pathway like formidable
cliffs or fallen trees.

Each of us has made promises to God
    and had our own crosses to bear.
Each of us has had to shake off
    the claws of the devil and choose righteousness.
And each of us has walked away from the wreckage
    or has stridden side by side with Death.

In the marathons of our lives, we have lived
    through the torments of the bully, lost jobs,
    or used the language of the beggar.

Who among us has not known the famine of the heart and soul,
    letting doubts reign?
We have survived unrelenting storms of faithlessness,
    or been forsaken by friends or those we've loved.
And we have lost our health, buried our dead,
    and mourned our lost selves.

I bear witness the Lord knows
where we have been, pulling back
the layers of despair and filling
the emptiness that's left over
with hope.

I promise that with the Lord
our grieving, suffering, and
heaviness of heart
will be but a short sojourn.

Joy comes like the beaming sun in the morning
and we will feel our souls break wide open
and praise Him.

I ATTEST THAT GOD LOVES ALL HIS CHILDREN

Michael Shoemaker

From the swollen banks of the Congo
to the flooded rice fields in South Vietnam
to the boy who waters down the dust
at the beginning of the day
in a Guatemalan open-air market
to the schoolgirl who opens
her umbrella on an unusually rainy day
while waiting at a bus stop in Adelaide, Australia
to the roofer from Mumbai, India who hastily patches
the holes with mud before the monsoons come
to the farmer from Northern Ireland
who with an oath stamps mud off his boots
to the lady who for fifty years
has softly cooed and comforted
butterflies in the cool mists
of her vegetable and flower gardens
in Bellingham, Washington
to the man who shivers and leans into the sleet
in the grey reality of a fishing boat
undulating in the choppy storm
near Norway's coast in the North Sea
to the group of children from Tibet
who launch homemade teetering kites
into sprinkling rain and wind
all are in reach of God's mercy—
"That I will give you the rain
of your land in his due season,
the first and the latter rain..."
   (Deuteronomy 11:14)

CHRIST-CENTERED THEMES

WALKING WITH THE LORD

Michael Parker

I am walking with the Lord...

When I seek after Him in the valley of faith and prayer.
When I can recognize what is and isn't important in my life.
When I align my will with God's will.
When I love Him for His sacrifice and death on my behalf.
When I place spiritual boundaries (such as how, when, or
    where I worship) in my life.
When I read and ruminate on the Scriptures.
When I am in reconciliation with Him.
When I forsake the raw and wild man that I am.
When I remember, first and foremost, I am
    His ambassador.
When I let Him prevail in my life.

OH, HOW I NEED THEE

Michael Shoemaker

Help of the helpless, Lord.   Do not know how to speed up the healing of scars on my left knee from a bike accident.   Unsure how to advise a friend on how to find a better job.   What is going on that my car's engine service light is coming on again? Where should I take it in to get it checked out?   I wonder why these tomato plants aren't sprouting. Is it too hot, windy or dry or is it just my inattention in caring for them?   Should a supervisor call out and make fun of a co-worker in front of others? What can I do about it, if anything?   Why do I keep on losing my temper again, again, and as You know, again, when it is the last thing that I want to do? I hope this seventy-times-seven thing is really working.   I thought by my age I would be wiser, kinder and gentler and yet I wonder why so often it doesn't appear to be working out that way.   What can I do to help the poor when their daily calls for help threaten to engulf and overwhelm me? How can I help them if I am not always well?   What can I do with the sorrow I feel over losing wild places of reflection, animals, plants, water and air?   Will Isaiah's prophecy of the desert blooming as a rose come to pass? What do I need to do so I don't tire of the desert and move out before Christ comes again?   Refresh, oh refresh me, Dear Father.   Do I need to worry about pruning those future rose bushes now? Don't know how to help family members who are far and away. No guesses are left of how to stop wars, hate and famine in this multiple-spinning-plate world of ours.

How well You listen to what my heart says: words can't express
and lips can't form!

I bring these to Thee. You know all things. Help of the helpless,
Lord, abide with me.
Peaceful Presence is power enough.

Because of Thee, I've got Love like an ocean in my soul.

Imperfect prayers are not ineffectual.
They move the mightiest of mountains.

CONSIDERING THE MASTER'S LOVE
Michael Parker

When He commanded His followers
to "love one another, as I have loved you."

When He came upon Martha and Mary
after Lazarus had died and He wept with Mary.

When He blessed and served the poor,
the sick, and the afflicted.

When He physically healed others and
offered encouragement or forgiveness.

When He raised the daughter of an ardent and faithful Jairus
from her deathbed as if she had sleepily arisen from a dream.

When He talked with the Samaritan woman at the well
even though Jews avoided Samaritans because
of a hundred-year-old feud.

When He broke bread with Matthew, the Publican,
even though Publicans were hated by the Jewish people.

When He served His enemies by feeding them,
teaching them, and showing tenderness toward them
even when He knew they would later kill Him.

When He admonished His disciple Peter
to forgive his brother "seventy times seven."

When He refused to accuse the woman
caught in adultery, instead saying to the angry mob
"he who is without sin among you, let him cast the first stone."

When He invited the devoted man to stretch forth
his deformed hand, and upon doing so
his hand was healed whole.

When He showed compassion upon the woman
who touched the fringe of His garment and
was immediately healed from her twelve-year-long
flow of blood.

When the apostle John summed up the feelings of millions
when he wrote in his first epistle
"We love Him, because He first loved us."

JESUS, O KINSMAN REDEEMER

Michael Parker

Jesus, O Kinsman Redeemer, how You noticed my weaknesses and are helping me transform like a butterfly to inspirit these frailties until they are my strengths.

Jesus, O Kinsman Redeemer, how You saw what I lacked, as if I were a cracked bowl, and filled the cracks with molten gold to make my soul not only whole but substantially new-like and beautiful.

Jesus, O Kinsman Redeemer, how You witnessed my sense of worthlessness and loved me even the more.

Jesus, O Kinsman Redeemer, how You observed I had walked away from You, yet searched and rejoiced when You found me, as if I were the lost lamb.

Jesus, O Kinsman Redeemer, how You perceived my heart was broken and You healed it with Your tenderness and care.

Jesus, O Kinsman Redeemer, how you recognized I was alone in my suffering and buoyed my spirit up with Your peace, comfort, and overwhelming love.

Jesus, O Kinsman Redeemer, how I am full of gratitude and adoration for Your steadfast presence in my difficult and bewildering life.

THE FIRST NOEL

Michael Shoemaker
an acrostic

Their sheep lay in fields
Heavenly light aflame
Eternal souls left to claim.

From Galilee's gleaming shores
In perfect healing ministry
Raising even the dead.
Scourged for no just cause
They hung Him on a tree.

Next day at the tomb
Only Mary saw Jesus
Extinguish death evermore
Life eternal to restore.

AN EXEGESIS ON FAMILIAR THEMES
Michael Parker

NIGHT AND DAY
Night, that long and dreary country,
the darkness of its clothes,
how it envelopes us in its arms,
carries us to the early hours
past midnight and we listen
to its impressible serenade
and sleep full of disordered dreams
(the labyrinthine garden of dreams)
and disconcerting nightmares.

Within the darkened house,
we ponder the visitation of spirits.
Spirits as appearances.
Spirits as messengers.
Spirits as ephemeral transients—
their weave of light and dark
that carry the echoes
of a melancholic, intractable past
or a sacred and well-lived life.

Outside, we follow the moon
and all her effulgent cycles—
waxing or waning.
The moon and her stars;
pinpoints of everlasting light;
children of the night;
the dance of stars,
lustrous constellations
and the river-like
Milky Way
luminous, brilliant,
and incandescent.
Surrounded,

we are in awe of all
God's vast creation.

After the illustrious dawn,
we live in quixotic days, light-heavy
nearly to the state of blinding.
We consider the sustenance
of our ordinary routines,
the exegesis of the sacred
in our lives, and the history
of the yet unwritten suffering,
the ennui, and the inextinguishable.
Sometimes there is relief, the remedy,
the beauty from ashes.
And, aid from the good Samaritans
who find us who suffer from things
along life's crossroads:
I'll carry you through your despair,
carry you through the thick of it
to the sunset of your life
(if God wills it)
that will bring relief from all
your suffering.

THE SEASONS
When the sun leaves his northern house
for warmer climes, winter enters—
winter and all its barrenness,
the skeletal trees and
fearsome Arctic storms
bringing snow and freezing rain
and how we shiver
even behind the walls and windows
of our houses.

Spring becomes the metaphor
of rebirth and the Lord's resurrection.
Spring, with all its newness,
the evidence of green flowers

and how they toil,
and even new windows to the soul.
We live the meaning of *carpe diem*
as taught by a loving grandfather,
long passed. Waves of gleaming
emotion at your evanescent memories,
and even the bittersweet symphony
of birdcalls through the rain,
wind and open skies.

Then arrives the invincible summer
with its heat and dancing mirages
in the body of the bone-dry desert.
Cumulus clouds float by, high in the sky.
The dog days of summer.
The moth to the infernal flame.
Hot sun and the inexhaustible search
for shade.
Burning up in cement-built cities.
Sun-kissed and scorching sand.
A whole wide world on fire,
a metaphor for the devil's country.

Then comes autumn and all
its vibrant colors. O, the great
orchestra of colors.
Brisk breezes, speaking leaves.
Poetry is alive in the air.
Long shadows from a mellow sun.
Harvest fields ready for the picking.
We consider gratitude and thanksgiving.
We count our blessings through
the season of the soul
and towering remembrances
in the slow, reluctant march
of time and the death of things.

DEATH

Death, *memento mori*,
speaks the murmuring mouths
of the dead: Life wills it
that we all will die.
So, we gaze life in the face,
day to day, knowing it is
tenuous.

Alas, the unfortunate passing
of things, the fateful transition
to the next life that we try
to acknowledge, commemorate
but this calamitous and
crushing state breaks us
wide open like eggshells.
The tragedy of death,
of fading away where we
forfeit beingness, and sometimes
doubt whether we slip away
into nothingness, lost
in translation.

Eternal rest.
O, death and all its layers
of silence on silence,
the deep trance of silence.

Yet, scripture encourages us
to never despair, but to be hopeful,
knowing there is a heavenly state
where our spirits travel
to wait for that future day
when the hosts of heaven
will herald the return of
the Savior.

Death cannot remain in power.
Did not a mournful Jesus
call forth Lazarus from
his cave of dirt
and bring forth the daughter
of Jairus from her bed of death
and did not an Angel of the Lord
roll back the round stone
allowing Mary and Mary Magdalene
to see the empty tomb of Christ
on the morning of the third day?
To this indubitable day,
His followers, like you and me,
delight in and rejoice.

Veni, vidi, vici!

"And death shall be no more;
Death, thou shalt die."

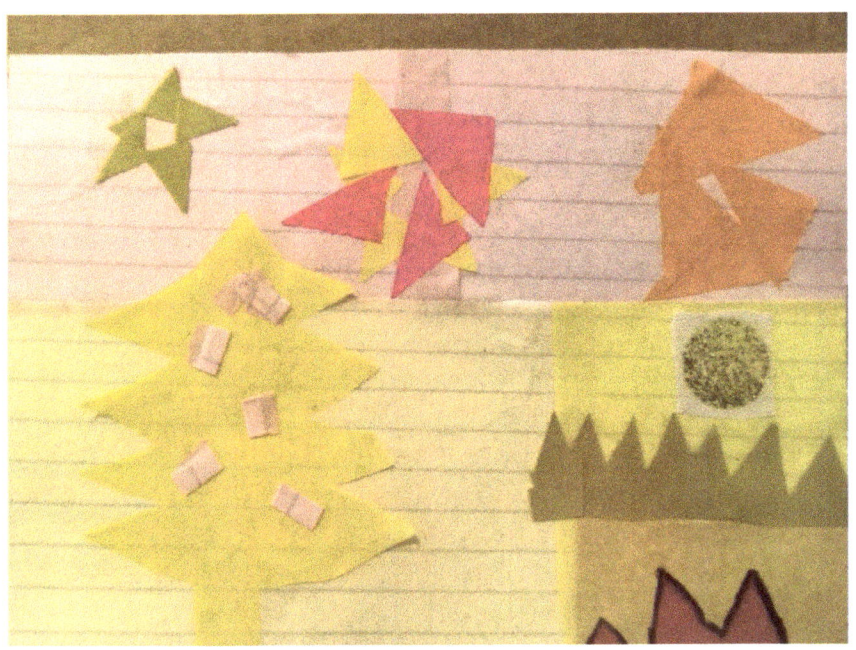

"Cascade Mountains." Artwork by Michael Shoemaker

SABBATH DAY

Michael Shoemaker
a sijo

The tree You hung on,
   lives Sabbath day anew to birth and growth;
its fruits' blossoms spring up bright and true,
   waking up to everlasting life and salvation's song.
Dear Savior, forgive me now my trespassed sins,
   rescue my royal birthright as a Beloved Son of God.

JAMES, THE BROTHER OF JESUS

Michael Parker
a triptych

1
When you are young
sharing a space
in the humble house
with your brother,
you're cognizant
of your differences.

When the lamp is lit
you see him pray

eyebrows so laden
forehead so illuminated
like a morning
in light.

You see the yearning
through his body
waiting for God.

You've spied angels
with the voices
of a thousand
rushing rivers
grow long wings
about him, enter
the spiral, ascending
to leave his side
burning through
the distance
and sound.

The angels do not minister
to you.

2
When people see you do they say
"You are your Father's son"?
Or, do they say "I see some
of Jesus in you"?

Though in awe of His qualities,
do you abscind yourself
from Jesus' perfect
beingness?

And does this knowledge cause you
to transform your quiescence
into mindfulness rather than
vindictiveness, (that ugly creature
that lurks in the core of all our souls),
and give you the fortitude
and resolve to grow in wisdom
and compassion
like your brother?

3
The days and nights have quickened like ferocious comets
and destiny will not cease until it has built that final act:

Your mother has rushed to Calvary to sit at His feet
and you still don't believe until He is

giving up the ghost or maybe it is later
when Jesus returns and speaks to you,

a resurrected being, the markings
of the spear and the nails, long iron spikes,

all but fresh in his side, feet and hands.
You remember this now, thirty years on,

falling from the pinnacle of a temple,
and how you would not deny your brother Jesus,
    who was called Christ,

stones flying at you before you even landed
at the feet of the inflamed mob.

JESUS IS

Michael Parker

A pure, unspotted lamb.

The thoughtful shepherd, who calls His sheep by name.

The unleavened bread we break and eat when we hunger.

The water we drink when we thirst.

The light, not unlike a lighthouse above the harbor, guiding ships safely in.

The sturdy grapevine which gives sustenance to its immutable branches.

The doorway to our hope and aspirations.

The path on which we follow with promise.

The truth we practice, obey, and observe.

The life that gives the fallen soul longing and faith in the eternities.

And, the resurrection that assures our life after death is secure,
>   that helps us anticipate our triumph over good and evil, and
>   the possibility of eternal life with God a joyous reality.

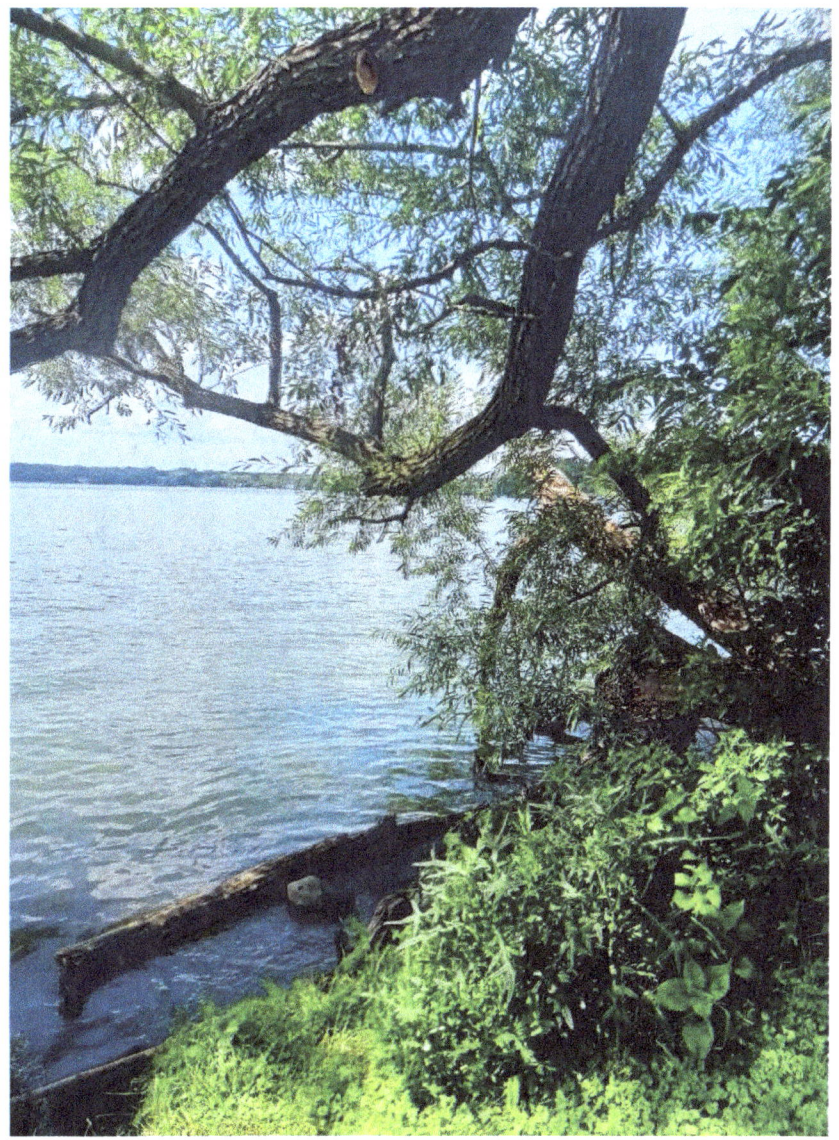

"Looking Out On Lake Mendota." Photography by Michael Shoemaker

RELIEVING PAIN FOR PAST ACTIONS

Michael Parker

You and I, fellow disciples, commit wrongs
(sometimes without our knowing it)
that wound our spirits, wound other souls,
take us further away from home,
and exhaust the supply of light within us.

At these times, our internal GPS is off-kilter.
The path heavenward is not straight ahead.
We must take an abrupt U-turn,
make a course correction, and
return to the Lord.

There are wastelands in our souls
that can be transformed into abundant gardens.

This act is repentance (*metanoia*).
It doesn't mean we have arrived home.
It doesn't mean we are suddenly perfect.
It's just a process of improvement we carry out each day.

This is how Christ's atoning work is completed in me:
By redemption—how the blood He spilt gave Him the power to
save me;
By restitution, which is the payment He restores to those I'm
indebted to;
By reclamation—how He repossesses my soul from the adversary;
By reconciliation, which is the sweet harmony produced
    between a forgiven me and my Lord;
and, by relief, the times when I feel the waves of guilt and despair
dissipate
    like the storms upon the sea swayed by the sweltering sun.

AUTUMN LEAVES ON THE SIDEWALK

Michael Shoemaker

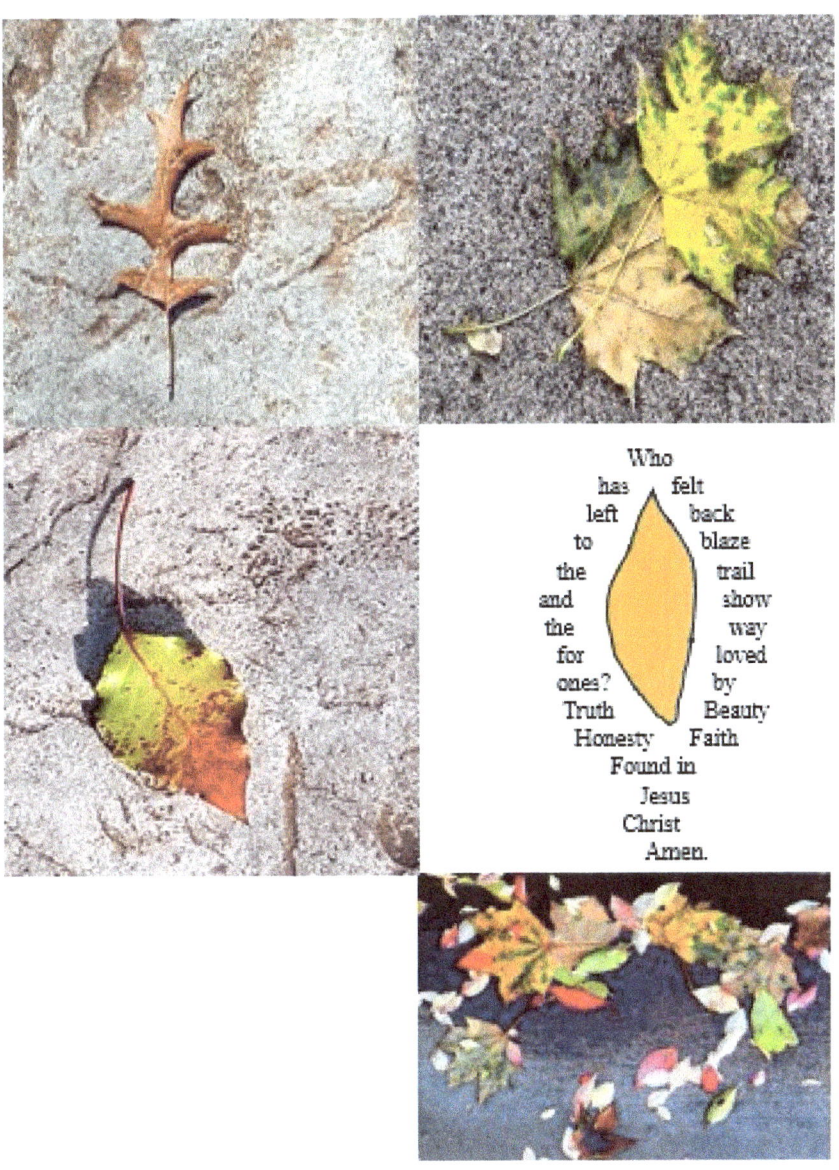

Who
has felt
left back
to blaze
the trail
and show
the way
for loved
ones? by
Truth Beauty
Honesty Faith
Found in
Jesus
Christ
Amen.

SEEING THE SEMBLANCE OF CHRIST

Michael Parker

For fourteen of my formative years
I grew up in Castle Valley, Utah—God's Country.

God was most assuredly in the castle-shaped
mountains, in its elevated cerulean sky
stretched wide over us, and amidst
the high desert landscape.
His presence was even in the poor,
nondescript mining towns banded
together by two-lane county roads.

I also found Him in other intimate places
such as within my home where we prayed,
in the protracted pews of the chapel
in the pioneer-like church house
where we worshipped, or within
the classrooms of the seminary
buildings adjoining the junior and
senior high schools where we were
instructed on the gospels and
His divine, effulgent son's teachings.

But something quite remarkable occurred
one Sunday morning on our drive
to Sunday School in Huntington
five miles away from our home.
My young siblings and I saw a man
appearing just like Jesus walking on
the opposite shoulder of the road
in the direction away from town.

Questions arose. Pleadings from
enthusiastic voices abounded:
"Let's pick Him up!"

My mother, who was driving the family van,
refused to turn around, stop and pick up
the mysterious stranger with
the living countenance of Christ
to our child-like eyes.

To this day, whenever I read
the experiences of Jesus, or think
of the impact of the Lord on this bleak
and battered life, I imagine Him
wandering less-traveled rural roads
of this far-reaching world and
how we passed Him by
one quiet spring morning
as the rose-colored sunrise
lifted off from the desert peaks
of Cedar Mountain and landed
on us and the tall castle-like walls
towering over the peaceful, arid
valley like loving and
protecting parents.

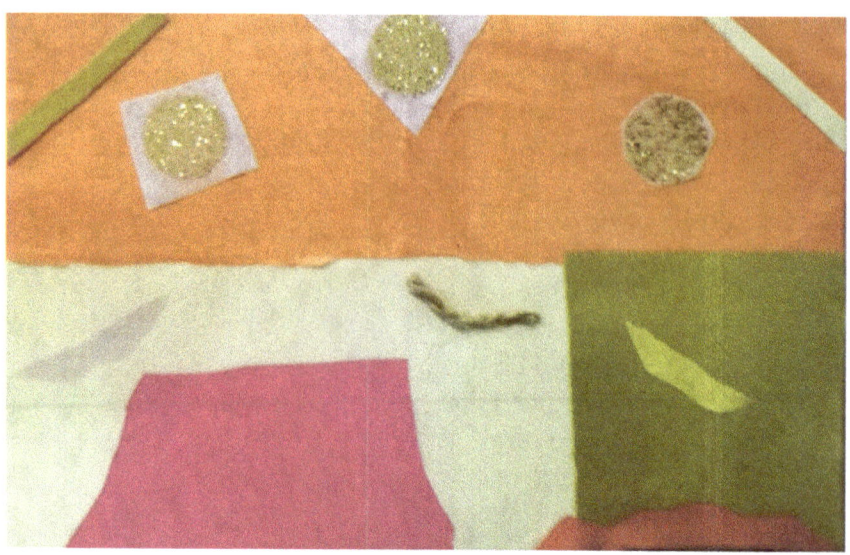

"Desert Solitude." Artwork by Michael Shoemaker.

THERE IS A PLACE

Michael Shoemaker
Here is the patience of the saints…and faith in Jesus Christ.
(Revelations 14:12)

It was hot.
It seems always to be hot these days.
Sweat was seeping into Tom's clothes
like rainwater looking for new pools
of expansion in which to stir, then rest.

We all had to stay at the airport gate #14.
It was seventeen minutes to boarding.
Babies were crying in Tom's bad ear,
his left one, and he winced in pain
He would have paid a day's wage to stop it.

A little dizzy from the heat and more
packed in and lined up in sections A, B, and C
like cattle waiting nervously to be loaded in train cars.
Tom doesn't read minds, but he knew they
wanted out of here and be anywhere else, right now.

He thought he might scream
or rage or swing his arms or
jump up and down or run and
never stop or faint and enjoy
the pleasure of release
it would bring.

Instead, a thought came into Tom's mind.
"Romans offered Jesus wine mixed with gall to drink."
He tasted it, Jesus did not drink.
Gall likely produced the easy way, an opiate-laced way out,
but He would have none of it.

Tom sat up having tasted in fantasy his ways out,
but he did not drink.
He would have none of it.
Tom drank a more bitter cup
and got home whole and in peace.

The clock patient counts down for all of us.
13, 7, 3, 0 minutes and home,
home of the saints,
company within Christ.

STARVING

Michael Parker

Thy words were found, and I did eat them; and thy word was unto me the joy and rejoicing of mine heart: for I am called by thy name, O Lord God of hosts. (Jeremiah 15:16)

In the midst of despair
and darkness,
I starved, longing
for light and joy.

I discovered it
reading the Word of God—
food for the heart,
poetry for the soul—
and pondering
each proverb,

I ate each word
whole and was satisfied
filled by
beauty and
holiness.

Rejoicing, I wear
Your name
ardently
like royal
robes,

my gracious
and beloved
Lord.

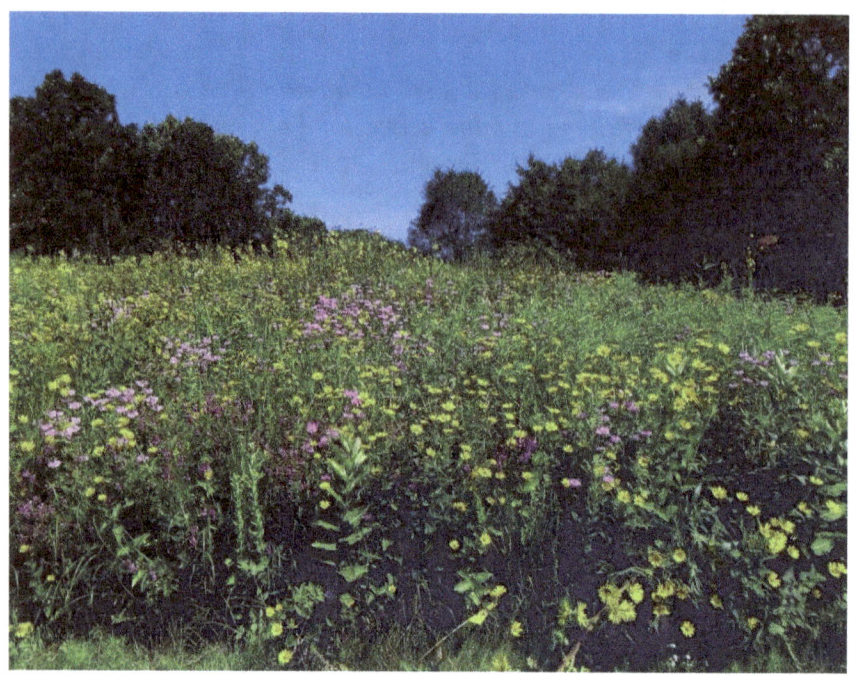

"Summer Wild Flowers." Photography by Michael Shoemaker

THE LENGTHS I WOULD GO

Michael Parker

O, the lengths I would go to follow Jesus.

I imagine I would be caught up in the news
of his deeds similar to the blind man
of Jericho, Bartimaeus, who had to have
overheard the stories about Him
prior to His coming so that when
the blind man heard the furor
of the approaching crowd and asked
what was happening, I like to believe my heart
would have leapt from my breast and
I, too, would immediately have cried out to Him
at the mention of His name—"Have mercy on me!"
And out of despair, as if I would lose
this rare and unbelievable opportunity,
I, too, would have shouted even louder
"Lord, have mercy on me!"

Would I have had the faith then like
Bartimaeus to ask to be healed?
I envision I would have and then Jesus,
recognizing my faithful desire,
would have granted it.

"Be prepared," I envision He would have
admonished me after the healing.
"Open your eyes," "See the needy,"
and "Minister to them in My name."
I foresee hearing His words embolden
this new man. Grateful, ardent, devoted,
and due to a change of heart for being healed,
I would pursue Him with such urgency
just like one of His impassioned disciples.

"[For] whosoever believeth in Him should not perish, but have eternal life." (John 3:15)

"Awake! awake! let the nations hear Jehovah's firm decree,
To abolish sin, and usher in The world's greatest jubilee." -
Eliza R. Snow- magnificent Christian Utah Poet

THE WORLD'S GREATEST JUBILEE

Michael Shoemaker

When Jesus comes again
what will happen then?

Will he know and feel
how to comfort and heal
with compassion
whatever besets
my neighbor's dog
that causes him
to bark every night
all night?

Will we sit   side by side

looking into   a mirror

and will He say,   "What do you see?"

"You and me,"   again, "What do you see?"

"my potential,   what You see in me,"

again, "What do you see?"   "love eternal, worlds without end,"

is that what will take place then

when He truly comes again?

THE SACRED STRAINS OF PEACE

Michael Parker

And the peace of God, which passeth all understanding, shall keep
your hearts and minds through Christ Jesus (Philippians 4:7).

When you and I open our souls and speak of peace,
we speak of the peace within ourselves—
the serenity abiding within us
(enjoying tranquility, wholeness, and restfulness)
or even the peace and satisfaction
of achieving a lofty goal.

We speak of the peace existing between
the bonds of friendship, husband and wife,
or even within the family;
of the peace we develop between the pleasant
relationship with other people—
living in harmony with them.

We speak of the tangible affinity between
countries—the absence of conflict or war;
and we speak of the peace of our sound
and invaluable relationship alive with God.

Peace exists figuratively to me, as well—
peace as a blessing of birds chirruping
in the forest of trees;
peace as the falling of water that dispels
the abundance of muck and misery in our lives;
peace as the invitation to see heaven;
peace as bestowing tenderness, as if by a kiss;
or even peace as kindness, bringing to those we love
blessings of loving-kindness.

So, softly raise the sacred strains of peace.
For the peace of Christ will help you persevere
your own pain; help you understand you are

no longer lonely in your suffering; and assist
you to better minister to the others
who suffer just like you.

CHRIST-CENTERED HAIKU

Michael Shoemaker

true vine
we abide in thee
— glorying in the Father
(Jn 15:1)

God's sweet-smelling savor
raises lovingkindness
to lasting grace
(Ep 5:2)

the chief cornerstone
builds a foundation
that will not fall
(Ep 2:20)

Woman, behold Thy Son!
Entrusting thee
to His disciple
(Jn 19:26)

rock of offence
I receive Thy Word
with open heart and hands
(Is 8:14)

Christ, our Passover
from evil pressing
destruction's deliverance found
(1 Cr 5:7)

little sanctuary
Son of the Most High God
— big relief
(Ec 11:16)

God also hath highly
exalted Him, with a name
above all
(Ph 2:9)

fear of the Lord
His judgments too
sweeter than honey
(Ps 19:9-10)

pattern of good works
let us follow Thee
in holy confidence
(Titus 2:7)

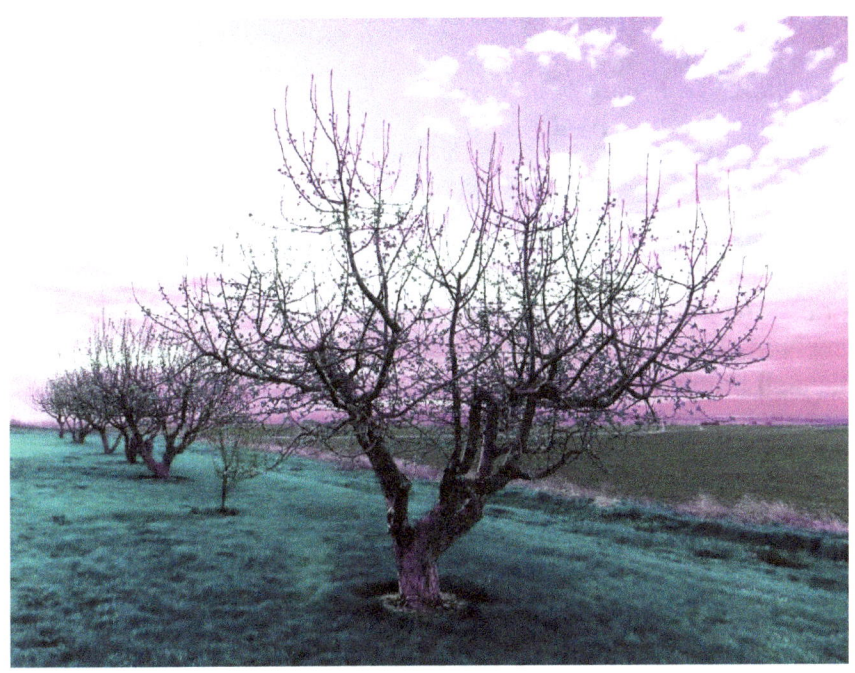

"From Here to Eternity." Photography by Michael Shoemaker

IF ANY MAN BE IN CHRIST

Michael Parker

Therefore if any man be in Christ, he is a new creature: old things are passed away; behold, all things are become new. (2 Corinthians 5:17)

If any man be in Christ (for example,
if they follow His commandments,
praise His holy name, or stand as
eye-witnesses of His Majesty)
then all things become new,
like the sapling rises from the maple;
the mainstem is fed from fresh tributaries;
the lamb is born from the sheep;
or the fawn from the white-tailed deer.

The teenager who testifies openly
of Christ to his friends;
the new mother who sings hymns to Him
as her sickly infant fights for her life in ICU;
or the faithful Father who demonstrates his
love for the Lord in front of a co-worker;
all of these become new creatures
in Christ.

What do you or I do to show our adoration
of the Lord? And better still, day after day,
or hour upon hour, how do you or I
consistently confirm Christ lives
in us?

Proclaim He lives!

HOW

Michael Parker

Love How I love the Savior How you How we hang upon His words like grapes to a vine How thirsty with need How we need to drink from the living waters How water flows from its source and becomes a river that flows to the ocean How that is a metaphor How the gospel of Christ moves through us like the rivers of life How His grace saves How His love feels How full of happiness How much joy and elation How it burns in the heart like an all-consuming fire How enraptured How enamored How transformed How indebted How Christ's mercy heals the distance between us and God How He sees us How He welcomes us like the Lost Sheep How He pardons us How He forgives us when we wrong Him or others How tender How caring How loving How He envelopes us like a thick coat or wings around her chicks How we are moved to tears How great He is How majestic How blessed is His name How He invites us to follow Him How we pick up our crosses and follow How He asks us to be latter-day disciples How we kneel at his punctured feet, weep, and cry out "Lord!"

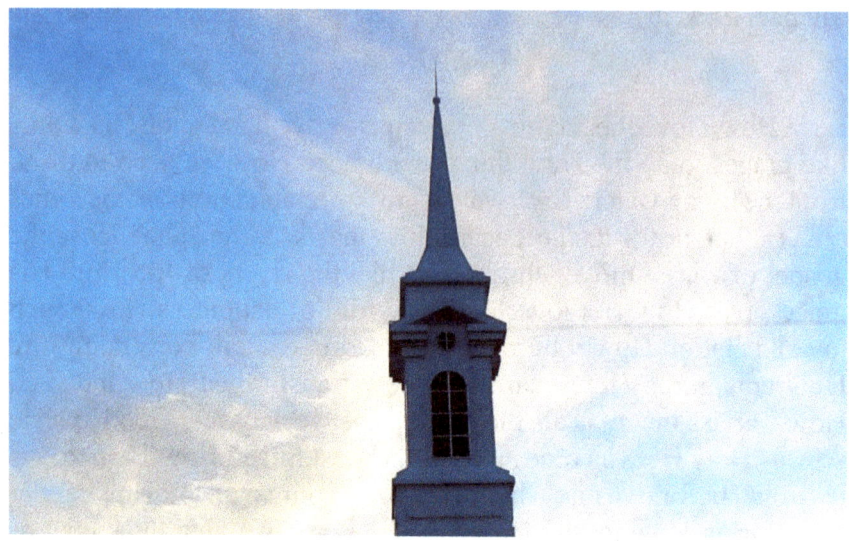

"Steeple at Sunrise." Photography by Michael Shoemaker

I AM THE SON MY FATHER RAISED TO STAND FOR CHRIST

Michael Parker
after Margo Tamez

when I listen closely to the susurration of things—
the brisk autumn wind and how the desiccated leaves
skitter across the city's driveways, sidewalks and streets —
and prepare my heart for the terminal decaying
of all things beautiful brought on by
this monomaniacal season

when I have been raised to have a sober character
to withstand the muck and refuse thrown my way

when I have been taught to observe and transcribe
the turning of a great people away from
goodness, light, love, aspiration,
and righteousness

when men lose their ears to lies and deceitfulness

when sterling men become enraptured by the wiles
of the men and movements who do the bidding
of the adversary

when I have become designedly determined
to win the race, break the record of the marathon,
and respectably defend the veracity and
truth of a Savior

when I must nourish quietude

when I must translate the turn of phrase and
emphasize what's holy between the lines

when my revered Father has passed on
and I must follow in his footsteps—
fight against the darkness,
fulfill God's will,
wear His impenetrable armor and
mantle of honor and virtue,
and shine Christ's existence like the glowing
city on the hill.

A PORTRAIT OF MY SAVIOR

Michael Parker

He is the healer, He is the counsellor, He is the carpenter, He is the teacher, He is the good shepherd, He is the master, He is the mediator, He is the bread of life, He is the sacrament of my soul, He is the bridegroom, He is a mighty fortress, He is an indomitable sanctuary, He is the cornerstone, He is the eye of the storm, He is the water in the well, He is the living water, He is the fountain of life, He is the balm of Gilead, He is the dayspring, He is the king of kings, He is the monarch of hope, He is the potter, He is the lamb, He is the exemplar, He is the God of miracles, He is the way and the truth and the life, He is the author and finisher of my faith, He is the morning star, He is the light of the brilliant map of stars, He is the light of the world, He is the rock, He is my rock, He is the vine, He is the fruit of the vine, He is the word, He is the Christ, He is the redeemer, He is Alpha and Omega, He is.

MICHAEL PARKER & MICHAEL SHOEMAKER

ABOUT MICHAEL PARKER

Michael Parker's poems and book reviews have appeared in *PoetsArtists, MiPOesias, Moss Trill, Littoral Magazine* (UK), *Dialogue, Blue Fifth Review, New Letters Literary Magazine, Literary Revelations Journal*, and elsewhere. The chapbook, *When the Wolves Come After You, Hang On*, co-written with Pris Campbell, was published in 2017. His poetry collection *Divining* 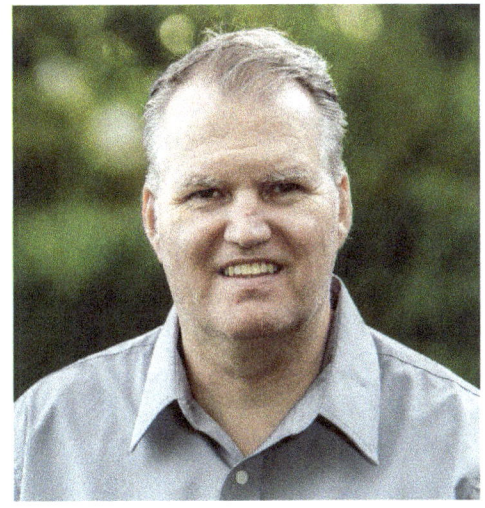 *the Spirits in the House of the Hush and Hush* won the Utah State Poetry Society's Book of the Year Award in 2021.

The latest collection *Sacred Strains of Praise* was the brainchild of Michael Shoemaker. Just over a year ago, Shoemaker asked Parker if he would like to co-author a collection of Christian-based poetry with him and Parker wholeheartedly agreed. "What a great opportunity it would be to write and compile poems that would both help me and those who read the collection praise and worship the Lord."

Parker is the President of the Utah State Poetry Society. You can contact him via his website, www.michaeldavidparker.com. He and his dear family live in Utah.

ABOUT MICHAEL SHOEMAKER

Michael Shoemaker is a husband, father and Christian who depends on grace every day, hopes in a glorious resurrection and trusts in the enabling and redemptive power of Jesus Christ. He is a poet, photographer and writer from Magna, Utah where he enjoys looking out on the Great Salt Lake. Michael is sharing his poems and photography in *Sacred Stains of Praise* to lift the lonely, encourage the weary 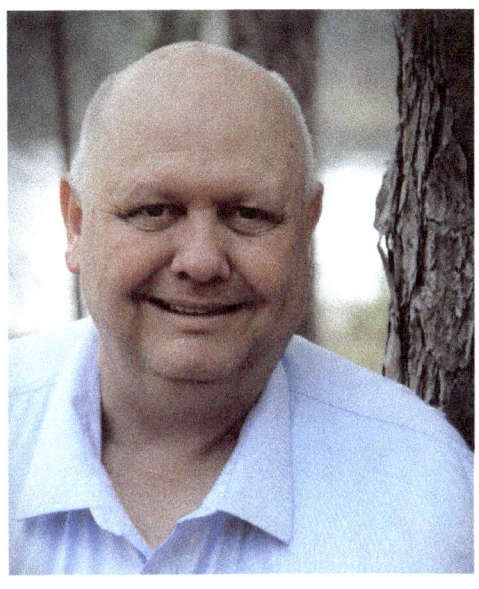 and provide healing that comes through the beautiful creations of God around us.

Michael is the author of three poetry/photography collections. His works have appeared in *The Christian Courier*, *Valiant Scribe*, *The Clayjar Review*, *Today's Living Christian Magazine*, *Spirit Fire Review*, and a featured interview with *Go! Christian Magazine*. He received a Living Waters Award in Poetry at Blue Lake Christian Writer's Conference and is a three-time nominee to the Best of the Net Anthology Awards. His website is at https://michaelshoemaker.crevado.com/.

DISCUSSION GUIDE FOR SMALL GROUPS OR INDIVIDUAL REFLECTION

1. Why do you think the authors chose *Sacred Strains of Praise* as their title?

2. In what way do the poems in *Sacred Strains of Praise* strengthen or embolden your faith?

3. What do you think is the significance of the authors opening and closing the poetry collection with the sections **Searching for God** and **Christ-Centered Themes**?

4. What are some of the universal themes you glean while reading the section **Life's Enduring Journey**?

5. What are your thoughts after reading the poem *The Goats and the Bees* from the section **Life's Enduring Journey**? How would you cope if faced with the same or a similar decision the narrator faced? How does guilt inhibit us from our connection with the Lord? How do regret and shame prevent us from healing and blessing other's lives?

6. Which photographs in this collection stand out to you? How does the use of photography enhance the meaning of the poems?

7. After reading the poem *Considering How We Connect With God*, ponder on the ways you have found to connect with God. Have these ways changed recently or over the years? Ask a close friend or family member how they connect with God and what blessings they have seen being closer to God.

8. While the subjects of haiku are often season, time of day, and the dominant features of the landscape, why do you think it was selected as a poetic form to praise Jesus Christ in this collection? How can thinking about Jesus Christ and His attributes from different perspectives help us to come to know Him better?

9. Once completed with reading the poem *Beside the Still Waters*, consider what role Scripture study and prayer have led you to be beside still waters. What steps may you feel inspired to take in you life that will help you to more fully come unto Christ?

10. How do you come to know what you know? How can you grow to trust what you learn and then know? After reading *On Knowing*, you may want to consider writing down your thoughts in a journal or diary.

11. After reading the companion poems *Maxine and Irene* and *A Feat of Charity at Christmas* from the section **Life's Enduring Journey**, how do the anonymous deeds of Maxine, Irene, and the narrator's family help you reflect on and teach you about charity, which is defined as the highest form of love. In what ways have you been the beneficiary of lovingkindness from others?

12. Think about the poem *I Attest that God Loves All His Children*, the last poem in the section **Life's Enduring Journey**. How does this poem movingly teach us about the reach of God's love? Write down the ways you know you are loved by God. List the ways you have felt God's presence in your life.

13. Read the poem *What the Chittering of the Grackles in the Yard Reveal to Me*. When has nature influenced or taught you about your divine worth or place in the world? Even though the poem is directed at the narrator, in what ways does it inspire you?

14. Consider the poem *If the Word of Christ Dwells in you Richly, Sing*. How do singing hymns and spiritual songs help you worship and praise the Lord? Think about the narrator's experience singing hymns with the group. How does singing to the Lord help you overcome your fears and be courageous to praise the Lord in front of strangers or even friends and family?

15. Upon reading the Scripture Jeremiah 15:16 used for the poem *Starving*, from the section **Christ-Centered Themes**, what ways have you been nourished by the word of the Lord? In what ways does the poem speak to your own experience of hungering for the words of the Lord?

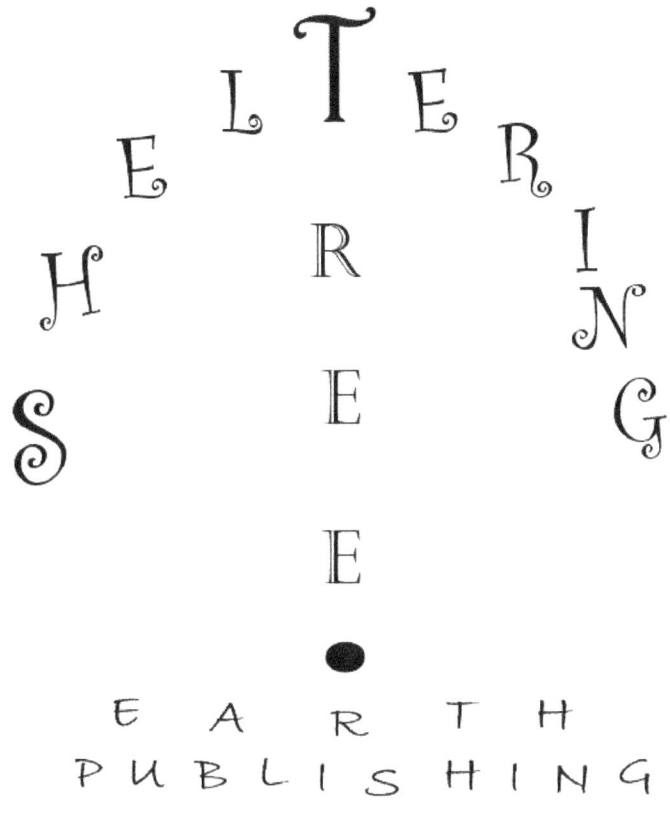

SHELTERING TREE EARTH PUBLISHING

ShelteringTreeMedia.com